KILLER PIES

Library of Congress Control Number: 2006928622

ISBN-10: 1-932855-57-2
ISBN-13: 978-1-932855-57-9

Cover Photograph: Mark Thomas/Jupiterimages

Killer Pies: Delicious Recipes from North America's Favorite Restaurants is produced by becker&mayer!, Bellevue, Washington.
www.beckermayer.com

Design: Kasey Free
Editorial: Kate Perry
Production Coordination: Shirley Woo
Project Management: Sheila Kamuda

10 9 8 7 6 5 4 3 2 1

Manufactured in China.

Chronicle Books
85 Second Street
San Francisco, California 94105

www.chroniclebooks.com

KILLER PIES

STEPHANIE ANDERSON

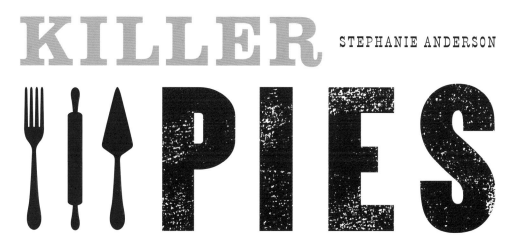

Delicious Recipes from North America's Favorite Restaurants

CONTENTS

6 INTRODUCTION
8 PIES 101

Northeastern U.S.

10 WALNUT CREAM PIE, Moody's Diner
12 COFFEE BUTTER CRUNCH PIE, The 1785 Inn
14 PEACH-BLACKBERRY PIE, Petsi Pies
16 PLUM-STRAWBERRY CRUMB PIE, Verrill Farm
18 PEAR-BLACKBERRY PIE WITH CARDAMOM, Marjolaine Pastry Shop
20 CONCORD GRAPE PIE, Arbor Hill Winery
22 OLD-FASHIONED APPLE PIE, The Little Pie Company
24 WILD BLUEBERRY PIE, Westville
26 WET-BOTTOM SHOOFLY PIE, The Famous Dutch Kitchen Restaurant
28 PONZIO'S PUMPKIN PIE, Ponzio's

Midwestern U.S.

30 DOOR COUNTY CHERRY PIE, Sweetie Pies
32 SOUR CREAM PLUM PIE, Cheyenne Ridge Outfitters & Lodge
34 SWEET APPLE PIE, Stagecoach Inn Bed & Breakfast
36 SOUR CREAM RAISIN PIE, Lange's Café
38 APPLE PIE, Around the Clock Restaurant & Bakery
40 PECAN PIE, Deerfield's Bakery
42 "MILE-HIGH" LEMON CHIFFON PIE, Stone's Restaurant
44 JOHNNY'S CAFÉ PECAN PIE, Johnny's Café
46 CHOCOLATE-COVERED CHERRY PIE, Just Pies
48 SISTER LIZZIE'S SHAKER SUGAR PIE, The Golden Lamb

Southern U.S.

50 STRAWBERRY-RHUBARB PIE, The Ham Shoppe
52 BOB ANDY PIE, Dangerously Delicious Pies
54 BANANA CREAM PIE, McEwen's on Monroe
56 LEMON CHESS PIE, The Morrison-Clark Inn
58 KAHLÚA PECAN PIE, Poogan's Porch
60 COCONUT MERINGUE PIE, Crystal Grill
62 COCONUT CREAM PIE, Blue Bonnet Café
64 FUDGE PIE, Ed & Kay's
66 KEY LIME PIE, Louie's Backyard
68 S'MORE PIE, Bayona

Western U.S.

70 SOUR CREAM RAISIN PIE, Lynden Dutch Bakery
72 GRANDMA'S CHOCOLATE PIE, Rose River Inn Bed & Breakfast
74 RASPBERRY CHERRY PIE, North Fork Store & Café
76 MISSISSIPPI COMFORT PIE, Inn at Schoolhouse Creek
78 CHOCOLATE PECAN PIE, Sweetie Pies
80 OLD-FASHIONED CHESS PIE, Walnut Café
82 APPLE PIE, The Famous Plaza Restaurant
84 MEXICAN CHOCOLATE CREAM PIE, The Border Grill
86 NEW MEXICAN APPLE PIE, The Daily Pie Café
88 PEACH PIE, Pie in the Sky

Canada

90 SADIE'S ALMOND CHOCOLATE PIE, Vi's for Pies
92 SASKATOON PIE, Black Cat Guest Ranch
94 MANITOBA MAPLE-WALNUT PIE, Just Desserts Café
96 FROZEN PEANUT BUTTER PIE, Aberdeen Mansion
98 RASPBERRY-RHUBARB PIE, Cascadia Bakery
100 MAPLE SYRUP PIE, Restaurant Aux Anciens Canadiens
102 VERY BERRY PIE, Heartwood Bakery & Café
104 LEMON MERINGUE PIE, Wanda's Pie in the Sky
106 NIAGARA FRESH FRUIT PIE, The Pie Plate Bakery & Café
108 APPLE-CRANBERRY GALETTE WITH CARAMEL, Sweet Caroline

110 INDEX
112 ACKNOWLEDGMENTS & IMAGE CREDITS

CANADA

NORTHEASTERN U.S.

MIDWESTERN U.S.

WESTERN U.S.

SOUTHERN U.S.

N
W E
S

INTRODUCTION

I have a confession to make: I was not always a pie person. I'd eaten pie, of course, but I'd never really appreciated pie. And, tragically, I'd never baked one. Pie was not a big deal in my family. Sure, we ate pumpkin pie at Thanksgiving like every other American family, and my mother has always requested a cherry pie for her birthday, instead of a cake. But with my Italian relatives we ate cannoli and other pastries, and my grandmother made cakes for special occasions. I just don't remember a lot of pie.

My childhood friend Christy and her family, however, were pie people. They lived down the street and had a large garden in their backyard in which they grew tomatoes, corn, onions, lettuce, and rhubarb. I had never seen rhubarb before and was intrigued by its deep-pink hue and celery-like stalks. The first time I ever tasted it was in an incredible pie Christy's mother had baked.

Years later, after we'd grown up and moved out of our childhood homes, Christy migrated to Montana. I lived with her for a few months after college, and one day, she baked an apple pie—not for a holiday or a celebration or gathering of some kind, but just because. Not that I complained, but I made a smart-alecky crack about her having become a pioneer woman since she'd moved from suburban Pennsylvania to the Wild West. But that pie was something else.

Since those bygone summers of Christy's mother's rhubarb pie, I have met other self-proclaimed "pie people" and developed my own theory about why people love pie so much. It's a simple hypothesis, nothing earth shattering: It's all about nostalgia. Pie reminds us of our youth, of a time when things were simpler. The pies we remember and love are the ones that were made by hand, from scratch, by people we remember and love: our mothers, our grandmas, our aunts, our kind neighbors. We didn't count calories or carbohydrates back then either, so there was never that twinge of guilt bouncing off the walls of our gustatory consciences. The rule was hard, fast, and nonnegotiable: You didn't turn down a slice of pie—ever.

The first pie I baked was a deep-dish apple pie. I

was exhausted after peeling the fruit, which is pretty much the first step. I'm not sure who was responsible for coining the phrase "easy as pie," but, at my first go-around, I took issue with it.

After I finished assembling the pie, I slid it into the oven and waited, clicking the oven light on every few minutes to check its progress through the glass door. When it finished baking, the wait for it to cool so I could slice into it was unbearably long. Finally, in all its golden-brown majesty atop a wire rack on my kitchen counter, it was ready. I'm pretty sure it was the best pie ever.

Pie is old-fashioned, and few foods have wound their way into our collective folklore and cultural land-scape as it has. Pie is a dessert that is designed to be simple, but it takes time, skill, and practice to make it well. This simplicity is what makes people adore this tried-and-true dessert, while the time and energy nec-essary to make a pie, which most of us don't always have, cause many to show surprise when you present a homemade pie.

Nothing, certainly not purchasing a store-bought pie, can replace this act of creation, of making some-thing with your own two hands, getting those hands sticky with dough, filling your house with the dizzying aroma of a pie's delightful sweetness, and turning a few, usually common items into something extraordinary. Think of how much time and experience, knowledge and skill the bakers in this book, who have generously shared their wonderful recipes, put into creating and culling their pie recipe collections.

People often say that cooking is an art and baking is a science. While this is certainly true—upsetting the balance of ingredients too much just won't work—there is definitely a lot of room for creativity. Play around with different flavors. Fiddle with ingredients and tech-niques a bit until you get the kind of crust and filling you love. And always remember that while there's little on this planet more perfect than a slice of fresh-from-the-oven pie, the journey is just as satisfying (and fun!) as that delicious destination.

Happy baking!

PIES 101

The Crust

Pie connoisseurs will tell you that the crust is the single most important element of a pie. It's what elevates a pie from so-so to out-of-this-world. Flaky is good; soggy is not. Dough recipes vary: Some use vinegar, which increases flakiness, while some don't. Some use lard, while others use shortening or butter or some combination of the three.

While many of the pie recipes included here provide instructions for making crust, some do not. In those cases, you may use the following recipe from Wanda's Pie in the Sky in Toronto, Ontario.

Pie Shell

$^3/_4$ cup (1$^1/_2$ sticks) cold unsalted butter, cut into $^1/_2$-inch pieces

2 cups all-purpose flour

$^1/_4$ cup sugar

$^1/_4$ teaspoon salt

$^1/_3$ cup ice-cold water

In a food processor or a large bowl, combine the butter, flour, sugar, and salt. Process or cut with a pastry cutter until the mixture resembles coarse meal and begins to clump together. Sprinkle with water, let rest for 30 seconds, and then process or cut again very briefly, just until the dough begins to stick together. Turn out onto a lightly floured board and press together to form a disk. Wrap in plastic and refrigerate for at least 20 minutes.

On a lightly floured board, roll the dough into an $^1/_8$-inch-thick 11- or 12-inch circle, then fit into a 9- or 10-inch pie plate. Trim the dough, leaving a 1-inch overhang, and fold under itself. Flute decoratively. Chill for 30 minutes.

For **double-crust pie dough**, double the ingredients and divide the dough into 2 disks. Wrap each in plastic and refrigerate for at least 30 minutes.

Leave the pie crust unbaked if your recipe calls for it, or pre-bake it: Preheat the oven to 400°F. Prick the crust all over with a fork. Line the crust with foil and fill with pie weights or dried beans. Bake for 15 to 20 minutes, then carefully remove the foil and weights or beans. For a **partially baked shell**, continue baking until lightly browned, about 5 minutes. For a **fully baked shell**, continue baking until golden brown, about 10 to 15 minutes more. Cool completely on a wire rack before filling.

Basic Bakin' Tips

★ Always use unsalted butter unless the recipe says otherwise. The butter should be cold. Ditto for lard or shortening. So should any called-for water—chill it by adding ice first, then remove the ice just before measuring. Some bakers even recommend sticking the fats in the freezer to make them easier to work with. Warm or even room-temperature fats make a sticky mess of your dough. And don't forget to chill the dough before rolling it out. Chilling relaxes the gluten in the dough and makes for a more tender, flaky crust.

★ How you add the fats to the flour makes all the

difference as well. Glopping a mound of butter, for instance, into a bowl of flour will result in, well, a mound of flour-covered butter, so slice the cold butter and fats into small pieces before adding them to the dry ingredients. (Using sticks of butter and shortening makes this easy.) Incorporate only a little bit of fat into the dry ingredients at a time by making a cutting motion with a pastry blender or a pair of knives. Do this until you've added all the fats and the mixture resembles coarse meal or peas. Don't overwork the dough, though. Small globules of fat should be visible.

★ Fluting, or crimping, which creates that familiar wavy edge, is a common technique and a way to make the edge of your crust both more decorative and stable. For a single-crust pie, trim the overhanging dough to a uniform inch (or less, depending on the recipe) and fold the dough under itself. For a double-crust pie, trim the bottom crust overhang to $1/2$ inch and top crust overhang to 1 inch; fold the top crust overhang under the bottom crust. Using your thumb and index finger of one hand, pinch the outside edge of the dough together while pushing in from the inside with your other index finger. You can also use a fork to make an indentation on the inside of each "flute." Continue fluting every $1/2$ inch around the rim.

★ Use excess dough to create other decorative crust designs, such as a braided or rope crust. Use the tip of a spoon or the tines of a fork to make scalloped-shaped or lined indentations.

★ The Little Pie Company in New York City shares this technique for making leaves out of dough:

Re-roll dough scraps to make 3 large diamond shapes, each about $2^1/2$ inches long, by cutting them out freehand or using a diamond-shaped cookie cutter. Use the back of a paring knife to make indentations in each diamond to simulate leaf veins. Brush the back of the leaves lightly with egg wash, then apply the leaves to the very top of the pie crust or filling, bending or twisting them slightly to give them a natural look. You can also cut out several small leaf shapes to affix in a ring around the crust.

★ Add pie weights or dried beans to the pie shell if you're pre-baking it (also known as baking "blind"). This holds the crust in place in the pan and prevents it from bubbling up.

★ Bake your pie in the bottom third of your oven. This will prevent the top crust from browning too quickly and before the bottom crust and filling are completely baked.

★ Be sure to cut slits or holes in the top of double-crust fruit pies to allow steam to escape. The general rule of thumb is that when the top is brown and the juices are bubbling, the pie's ready to come out of the oven.

★ Resist the urge to slice into a hot pie. It'll taste fine, but you'll end up with a falling-apart mess. Cooling the pie for a few hours on a wire rack—which allows for air circulation— makes the ingredients stick together, resulting in clean, neat slices.

★ Use a knife warmed in hot water—wiping off excess water each time—to cut your pie.

MOODY'S DINER

WALDOBORO, MAINE

Everything about Moody's Diner feels like a throwback to a bygone era, when family road trips were more about the journey than the destination, and when bliss could be found in a cup of coffee and a slice of pie. The New England family-run diner embraces its eighty-plus-year legacy, and according to its customers, happiness can still be found in a slice of tasty pie. But don't let the quaintness of this national icon of an eatery fool you—Moody's is serious about food. It has been featured in *Saveur* magazine, won a gold medal from the Culinary Hall of Fame, and was nominated for a Restaurant of the Year award from the Maine Restaurant Association.

Moody's is also serious about pie, particularly its delicious walnut cream and four-berry varieties.

True, patrons can belly up to diner favorites like meat loaf and apple crisp, but the pie is Moody's true claim to fame, in Maine and beyond. The diner's six pastry cooks work long hours, starting their shifts at three or four in the morning and working till two in the afternoon during the summer, when they bake sixty pies every day for eat-in and take-out customers. At Thanksgiving, they sell about two hundred pies to go. "Now, Waldoboro isn't a big metropolis or anything," says Dan Beck, Moody's manager and grandson of the founder. "To do that many pies for a small community is a lot." The beloved walnut cream pie has been featured in *Gourmet* magazine and was chosen by food gurus Jane and Michael Stern, authors of *Roadfood*, as one of America's Top Ten Pies.

Walnut Cream Pie

Crust

    1 heaping cup vegetable shortening

    3 cups all-purpose flour

    1 teaspoon salt

    3/4 cup cold water

Cut the shortening into the flour and salt until the mixture resembles coarse corn-meal. Add the water, a little at a time, until the dough just holds together; adding too much water will make the dough tough. Divide the dough into 4 equal parts; freeze or refrigerate 2 parts for later use. Roll out the remaining 2 parts on a floured surface, creating 2 single crusts. Fit each into a 9-inch pie plate and flute the edges.

Filling

    3/4 cup (1 1/2 sticks) margarine, melted

    1 1/2 cups sugar

    9 eggs

    3 heaping tablespoons all-purpose flour

    3/4 teaspoon salt

    1 1/2 teaspoons vanilla extract

    2 1/2 cups dark corn syrup

    2 cups milk

    2 cups chopped walnuts

Preheat the oven to 350°F. In a large bowl, beat together the melted margarine, sugar, eggs, flour, salt, vanilla, and corn syrup. Beat well, then stir in the milk. Spread 1 cup of nuts in each uncooked 9-inch pie shell. Pour the batter over the nuts and bake for 30 to 40 minutes. *Makes two 9-inch single-crust pies, with 2 additional single crusts.*

GENERAL BAKIN' TIP

★ To prevent spills, Moody's recommends pouring all but 1 cup of the filling into the pie shell and adding the remaining filling after your pie is transferred to the oven.

THE 1785 INN

NORTH CONWAY, NEW HAMPSHIRE

hen one thinks of a historical New England ski town, visions of snow-topped hills, rosy-cheeked people, and a dinner of warm, hearty food in front of a crackling fire spring to mind. Sound unbelievable? In North Conway, New Hampshire, this fantasy is actually a reality. Built in, well, 1785, the 1785 Inn has enjoyed a long tradition of providing locals and travelers alike with food and lodging. Becky Mallar, who owns the inn with her husband, Charlie, explains that the colonial house was "built by someone who fought in the Revolutionary War. You can still see the original hand-hewn beams, and we light the three original fireplaces nightly when it's cool enough."

Mallar, who hails from Michigan, always liked to bake and entertain, and she took cooking classes in the 1970s from Georges Perrier, famed chef of five-star Le Bec Fin. When she and her husband bought the 1785 Inn in 1983, she happily became the pastry chef and introduced one of the inn's best-loved desserts—the coffee butter crunch pie. "We keep it in the freezer, so it's like a frozen coffee mousse pie in a crunchy walnut-and-chocolate-chip crust," Mallar says. The pie was featured in an article in *Bon Appétit* and has gained a following over the years. She can hardly keep it in stock, and not just because customers keep ordering it. "Charlie sometimes sneaks a piece late at night," Mallar says. "It's his favorite dessert."

Coffee Butter Crunch Pie

Crust

- 1 package single-crust pie crust mix
- 1 ounce unsweetened chocolate, coarsely chopped then ground
- 1/4 cup packed light brown sugar
- 1 cup walnuts, finely chopped
- 1 teaspoon vanilla extract
- 1 tablespoon water

Preheat the oven to 375°F. Place the mix in a large mixing bowl. Stir in the chocolate, then the sugar and walnuts. In a separate bowl, mix the vanilla and water, then drizzle over the dry mixture. Stir briefly until crumbly. Line a 9-inch pie pan with aluminum foil and place the crust mixture into it, pressing it up the sides and into the bottom of the pan. Bake for exactly 15 minutes, then allow the crust to cool.

Filling

- 1/2 cup (1 stick) unsalted butter, at room temperature
- Scant 1 cup light brown sugar
- 1 ounce unsweetened chocolate, melted and cooled
- 2 1/2 teaspoons instant coffee powder
- 2 eggs

In a small bowl, use an electric mixer to cream the butter. Gradually add the sugar and beat on high speed for 2 to 3 minutes. Add the chocolate and coffee. Add the eggs 1 at a time and beat well. Pour the filling into the crust and freeze for several hours. When frozen, carefully take the pie out of the pan, remove the foil, and return the pie to the pan.

Coffee Whipped Cream Topping

- 1 pint heavy cream
- 1 tablespoon instant coffee, ground to a powder
- 1/2 cup confectioners' sugar

Whip all the ingredients together in a chilled bowl until soft peaks form and add to the top of your pie. Serve. *Makes one 9-inch single-crust pie.*

PETSI PIES

SOMERVILLE, MASSACHUSETTS

Renee McLeod first started baking as a young girl and hasn't looked back since. "I've been baking since I was eight or nine with my grandmother," she says. "I rolled out the pie dough." Baking pies became her full-time job when McLeod opened Petsi Pies in Somerville, Massachusetts, in 2003. Still, she hasn't forgotten bygone days when she just made pies for fun; even the shop's name is a tribute to her childhood nickname, Petsi. "I was supposed to be Peter," she explains.

From her tiny shop, McLeod and her staff bake all sorts of treats, including scones, coffee cakes, muffins, cookies, cupcakes, and a variety of both sweet and savory pies. Petsi Pies' peach-blackberry pie is McLeod's favorite summertime pie. The dessert combines the sweet juiciness of peaches and blackberries, the fragrant spiciness of nutmeg, and the fresh bite of lime. Even though the business is relatively new, it's quickly gained a devoted following. When attempting to put the atmosphere of Petsi Pies into words, McLeod had Laura, a loyal customer, describe it instead: "It's sunny and warm and the aroma is amazing," Laura exclaimed, then added to McLeod, "I'm your biggest fan!" McLeod thinks she's since found the right words to describe her bakery: "It's little, and we're here all day, dancing and singing."

Peach-Blackberry Pie

Filling

>   8 ripe peaches
>
>   4 cups fresh or frozen blackberries
>
> $\frac{1}{2}$ cup sugar
>
>   3 tablespoons cornstarch
>
> $\frac{1}{2}$ teaspoon ground nutmeg
>
>   1 tablespoon fresh lime juice
>
>   1 teaspoon grated lime zest

1 unbaked 9-inch pie shell (page 8)

Preheat the oven to 350°F. Blanch the peaches in boiling water for 1 minute, then place them in an ice bath. Remove the skins from the peaches, slice them (removing the pits), and mix the peach slices with the blackberries. Combine all the remaining filling ingredients, then stir into the fruit. Pour into the pie shell.

Crumb Topping

> $\frac{1}{2}$ cup packed light brown sugar
>
> $\frac{1}{2}$ cup all-purpose flour
>
>   **Pinch of salt**
>
> $\frac{1}{2}$ cup (1 stick) cold unsalted butter, cut into slices

Mix the brown sugar, flour, and salt in a food processor, then add the butter. Pulse until large, buttery crumbs form. Top the pie, leaving about 1 inch uncovered around the edge. Bake for 45 to 50 minutes, or until the filling juices are thick and bubbly. Cool at least 1 hour before serving. *Makes one 9-inch single-crust pie.*

GENERAL BAKIN' TIP

★ The key to this delicious pie, McLeod says, is using fresh, ripe peaches that are in season. You can tell if a peach is ripe by smelling it. The best ones smell very peachy. Never squeeze them—they bruise easily.

VERRILL FARM

CONCORD, MASSACHUSETTS

In 1918, Jennifer Verrill-Faddoul's grandfather started a dairy farm on a 140-acre plot of land in Massachusetts. Since then the farm has grown, both in size and reputation, while the surrounding area has become increasingly developed. "We're really one of the last farms in the area," Verrill-Faddoul explains. After selling their herd of dairy cows in 1990, the Verrill family decided to focus on growing produce. They replaced a roadside tent with a large stand, where they sell the farm's wares. Visitors can now purchase produce and other foods seven days a week, year-round—not just when the weather co-operates. The farm's mission is simple: "To nourish the body and soul of our customers by providing healthful food of superb flavor in surroundings of beauty." Evidently, the simple philosophy has caught on. The farm provides many Boston restaurants with fresh produce, and has been featured in *Boston* and *Gourmet* magazines.

While Verrill Farm is perhaps best known for its heirloom varieties of tomatoes and corn, one of its biggest draws isn't produce at all—it's the pies. As baking manager at the farm, Verrill-Faddoul makes and tastes her share of delicious pies, and her favorite is the plum-strawberry crumb variety. She likes baking with plums because they are "more dependable" than other fruits, such as peaches. While any type of plum will do, Verrill-Faddoul recommends using Santa Rosa plums for their bright orange color because, she explains, "They look pretty when they're cooked."

Plum-Strawberry Crumb Pie

Crust

2 1/4 cups all-purpose flour

1/4 cup granulated sugar

1 teaspoon salt

1 cup (2 sticks) cold unsalted butter, cut into cubes

1/4 cup cold water

Mix the dry ingredients and butter in a food processor, pulsing until crumbly. Add the water slowly and pulse until the dough comes together. Divide into 3 parts. Freeze or refrigerate 2 parts for later use. Roll out the remaining part and fit into a 9-inch pie plate.

Filling

4 1/2 cups chopped fresh plums

1 1/2 cups fresh strawberries, hulled and sliced

3/4 cup granulated sugar (less for sweeter plums)

3 tablespoons cornstarch

Mix all the filling ingredients in a bowl and pour into the pie shell.

Crumb Topping

1/2 cup (1 stick) cold unsalted butter, cut into cubes

1/4 cup packed brown sugar

1/4 cup granulated sugar

1 cup all-purpose flour

Preheat the oven to 375°F. Mix all the ingredients in a food processor or in a bowl with a pastry blender. Pulse or blend until crumbly.

Measure 2 cups of crumb topping (you might have some left over) and sprinkle onto the middle of the pie, gently spreading it across the filling and leaving about 1 inch bare around the edge. Be sure not to pack the topping down. Bake for about 50 minutes, until the juices are thick and bubbly. If the juices are too thin, bake for an additional 5 minutes. *Makes one 9-inch single-crust pie, with two additional single crusts.*

MARJOLAINE PASTRY SHOP

NEW HAVEN, CONNECTICUT

Marjolaine is an elegant European dessert that is made with layers of chocolate, hazelnuts, cream cheese, and puff pastry. Marjolaine is also the name of an elegant European-style bakery located a mile from the Yale University campus. This pastry shop, where patrons can grab a cup of coffee and a croissant in the morning or a sweet after-dinner treat, is both chic and homey. The bakery produces an array of gorgeous, delectable goodies, including wedding and birthday cakes, meringues, tortes, tarts, and the eponymous marjolaine. "We do everything but Italian pastry," says Rusty Hamilton, who refers to himself as the shop's "owner slash baker slash dishwasher slash most everything."

Hamilton learned to bake from Marjolaine's previous owner and, after twenty-five years of working at the bakery, tinkering with ingredients has also afforded him an invaluable education. "It's mostly a lot of trial and error," Hamilton laughs. "I guess you could say I'm self-taught." Adding to Marjolaine's cozy feel are the many pies the bakery produces, some of which feature unexpected twists on old favorites, such as the pear-blackberry pie. Hamilton's "trial-and-error" methodology paid off in this pie, which blends cool, subtly sweet pears and blackberries, the fingertip-staining summer favorite. Cardamom—a member of the ginger family and a staple in Indian cuisine—and cinnamon give the pie a warm, spicy kick.

Pear-Blackberry Pie with Cardamom

Filling

4 fresh pears, unpeeled

$1\frac{1}{2}$ cups fresh or frozen blackberries

1 teaspoon ground cinnamon

1 teaspoon ground cardamom

$\frac{3}{4}$ cup sugar

$\frac{1}{4}$ cup cornstarch

1 unbaked 9-inch pie shell (page 8)

Preheat the oven to 375°F. Core and slice the pears. Mix all the filling ingredients together well. Pour into the pie shell.

Crumb Topping

6 tablespoons sugar

$\frac{1}{2}$ cup pastry flour

$\frac{1}{2}$ teaspoon ground cardamom

2 tablespoons cold unsalted butter

Add the dry ingredients to a food processor or blender, pulse to combine, then add the butter. Mix until the topping comes together into crumbs. Add to the top of the pie, starting in the middle and spreading to $1\frac{1}{2}$ inches from the edge. Bake for 1 hour and 20 minutes, and let the pie cool before serving. *Makes one 9-inch single-crust pie.*

GENERAL BAKIN' TIPS

★ Bartlett pears work well in this recipe, and, if you prefer, the pie may be topped with a lattice crust instead of the crumb topping.

★ Rusty Hamilton recommends serving the pie a day after it has been baked so the flavors have time to meld together.

ARBOR HILL WINERY

NAPLES, NEW YORK

With a degree in pomology (fruit production and breeding), no wonder John Brahm grows a great grape. Brahm owns Arbor Hill Winery with his wife, Katie, in the Finger Lakes region of New York state, and their biggest draw is, of course, their critically acclaimed wine. They produce quite a few varieties from their grapes, including Chardonnay, Cabernet Sauvignon, and several dessert wines. In 1996, Arbor Hill became the first winery in the world to produce Traminette, a wine using a hybrid grape that Cornell University—Brahm's alma mater—spent thirty years developing.

But grapes are not just for wine; they're also perfect for jellies, jams, sauces, and pies, which people can purchase in the Grapery, the winery's retail shop. Arbor Hill's Concord grape pie, known to locals as the "famous Naples grape pie," is part of a beloved tradition that began in the 1960s at the historic Redwood Restaurant in Naples, New York. Now the town hosts an annual grape festival, drawing tens of thousands of visitors to the region. During a short six-week harvest period once a year, more than thirty thousand grape pies are made from Finger Lakes grapes, and for good reason: Brahm touts not only the grape pie's taste, but also its health benefits. The filling, made with both grape pulp and skins, boasts a high concentration of t-resveratrol, a disease-combating antioxidant.

Concord Grape Pie

Filling

8 cups fresh Concord grapes
1 teaspoon fresh lemon juice (optional)
6 tablespoons tapioca flour
2 cups sugar (more or less, depending on sweetness of grapes)
Dash of salt

Wash, drain, and stem the grapes. Remove the skins from the pulp and place in a saucepan. Place the pulp in a separate saucepan. Cook the pulp for 15 to 20 minutes, or until the seeds separate from the pulp. Add lemon juice if the grapes are very ripe; for less-ripe grapes, lemon juice is unnecessary. While the pulp cooks, simmer the skins in a small amount of water. Then run the pulp through a food mill and discard the seeds. Drain the liquid from the skins and set aside. Combine the skins, pulp, tapioca, sugar, and salt. Add a bit of the grape-skin liquid to the mixture if you prefer it more moist, then allow the mixture to cool.

2 rounds double-crust pie dough (page 8)
Milk or 1 egg white, for brushing

Preheat the oven to 400°F. On a lightly floured board, divide each round in half and roll each disk of dough into an 11-inch round. Fit 1 round into each of two 9-inch pie pans. Pour 3 cups grape filling into each pie shell, discarding any extra filling. Top each pie with a second round of dough, seal the edges, and brush with the milk or egg white, then pierce the crusts to create vents. Bake the pies for about 40 minutes, or until golden brown. Cool on a wire rack before serving. *Makes two 9-inch double-crust pies.*

GENERAL BAKIN' TIP

★ For a delicious treat, John Brahm encourages at-home cooks to use the grape filling in coffee cakes and strudels, and as a tart topping for ice cream.

THE LITTLE PIE COMPANY

NEW YORK, NEW YORK

After the Little Pie Company opened the doors of its first location on 43rd Street in Manhattan in 1985, it didn't take long for word to spread. The owners, Michael Deraney and Arnold Wilkerson, soon found their tiny storefront bakery inundated with New Yorkers clamoring for a whiff—and taste—of their mouthwatering fresh-baked pies. True to Wilkerson's dramatic background as a former actor, the Little Pie Company touts itself as a "theater of baking." Large windows allow passersby to watch bakers in tall white hats and crisp aprons cut fruit, make dough, and slide the pies into large ovens. Row after row of pies cooling on racks emit an aroma that is nothing less than intoxicating.

These days, Deraney and Wilkerson have two more locations in Manhattan—in Chelsea and in the Grand Central Station terminal—making it now triply difficult for New Yorkers to pass up their pies. Out-of-towners can also order from the company's website and take delivery of such favorites as sour cream apple walnut, Key lime, Mississippi mud, cherry, and Southern pecan pie. But the pie de résistance is their statuesque ten-inch-high old-fashioned apple pie. Deraney believes in the power of the pie and explains, "Pies are comfort food and stimulate a nostalgic vision of hearth and home. Our apple pie recipe is the flavor that I remember from my childhood."

Old-Fashioned Apple Pie

Crust

> 2 ½ cups unbleached all-purpose flour
>
> 1 tablespoon sugar
>
> 1 teaspoon salt
>
> ½ cup (1 stick) cold unsalted butter, cut into 1-inch pieces
>
> ½ cup cold lard or vegetable shortening, cut into 1-inch pieces
>
> 1 large egg, beaten
>
> ½ cup very cold water

In a large bowl, whisk together the flour, sugar, and salt. Add the butter and lard. (If using vegetable shortening, work in the butter first until it's the size of large peas, then add the shortening.) Using your fingertips, work the fat into the flour until the mixture forms pieces the size of peas. In a separate bowl, combine the egg and cold water. Add the egg mixture to the flour mixture in a fast, steady stream, stirring with a fork. Continue stirring until the flour is almost completely mixed in but the dough does not form a ball. Work in remaining flour with the heel of your hand. Divide the dough in half and shape into 2 disks. (There will still be pieces of butter and lard visible.) Wrap tightly in plastic wrap or waxed paper and refrigerate for at least 2 hours, or over-night. Roll out each disk and fit 1 pastry round into a 9-inch pie pan.

Filling

> 3 pounds (6 or 7) Golden Delicious apples, peeled, quartered, and cored
>
> ¼ cup firmly packed light brown sugar
>
> ¼ cup granulated sugar
>
> 2 tablespoons cornstarch
>
> ¾ teaspoon ground cinnamon
>
> ⅛ teaspoon grated nutmeg
>
> 1 ½ tablespoons fresh lemon juice
>
> 2 tablespoons unsalted butter, at room temperature

Preheat the oven to 425°F. Cut each apple quarter into 3 wedges. Put the apples into a large bowl. In a small bowl, whisk together all the remaining ingredients except the butter, and add to the apples, evenly coating them. Heap the filling into the dough-lined pie pan. Trim the bottom crust to a ½-inch overhang. Dot the filling with butter. Arrange the top crust over the apples, leaving a 1-inch edge. Fold the top crust under the edge of the bottom crust and flute the edges. Bake the pie until golden brown, 45 minutes to 1 hour. *Makes one 9-inch double-crust pie.*

WESTVILLE

NEW YORK, NEW YORK

Ivy Tack has been surrounded by pies her entire life. She helped her mother bake pies at home when she was a young girl, and later she made pizza pies at her family's pizzeria. Despite this background, Tack decided to eschew food service and enroll in pre-med courses in college, only to find herself working at a bagel bakery when she wasn't in class. She ultimately forewent medical school, and all it took was an episode of *Dessert Circus* with chef Jacques Torres to inspire Tack to tackle culinary school. She packed her bags and headed to New York, where she enrolled in the French Culinary Institute's pastry arts program.

In 2003, Tack became the pastry chef at the newly opened Westville, a tinier-than-tiny, nine-seat café in New York's West Village. Along with the restaurant's unique and healthy twists on standard American fare, Tack's pies and other goodies gained a strong following. *New York* magazine featured Tack in its prestigious annual "Best of" issue, voting her wild blueberry pie the city's best pie for 2003. Soon, Tack opened her own "freelance" baking company, Ivy Uppercrust Pastry, and customers contact her directly for her special-order desserts—though she continues to bake pies and other wares from scratch for Westville and other Big Apple eateries. Tack explains the appeal of her delectable treats: "My customers love my pies because they taste like what they tasted when they were little kids. My pies are like what your mother or grandmother made for you; they always bring you back to home again."

Wild Blueberry Pie

Crust

> 2 ½ cups all-purpose flour
>
> 1 ½ teaspoons kosher salt
>
> 1 cup (2 sticks) cold unsalted butter, cubed
>
> ¾ cup ice-cold water

Combine the flour and salt. Add the butter and mix with your fingers, a fork, or a stand mixer until the butter is in tiny, pea-sized pieces. Slowly add the water until the dough forms—you might not need the full ¾ cup. Form into 2 disks and wrap in plastic. Refrigerate for 1 hour or more, until cold.

Filling

> 5 cups fresh wild blueberries
>
> ¾ cup sugar
>
> ¼ cup all-purpose flour
>
> Grated zest and juice of ½ lemon

1 tablespoon unsalted butter
Milk, for brushing
Sugar, for sprinkling

Preheat the oven to 375°F. Put 2 ½ cups of the blueberries, the sugar, flour, and lemon zest and juice into a saucepan and stir to combine. Cook over medium heat until the mixture boils, stirring occasionally so the bottom doesn't burn. Boil for 3 to 4 minutes, or until the mixture thickens. Remove from heat and add the remaining blueberries, stirring to combine. Cool to room temperature.

Roll out each disk of pie dough and fit 1 crust into a 9-inch pie pan. Pour in the blueberry filling and dot with the butter. Cover with the second crust and crimp the edge to seal. Brush with milk and sprinkle with sugar. Bake until the crust is golden brown and the filling bubbles, 45 minutes to 1 hour. Cool to room temperature. *Makes one 9-inch double-crust pie.*

THE FAMOUS DUTCH KITCHEN RESTAURANT

FRACKVILLE, PENNSYLVANIA

Tom Levkulic never thought he'd be baking the same shoofly pies he ate as a boy growing up in a small town in rural Pennsylvania. The former engineer fell into the restaurant business quite by accident—he married into it. In 1971, Levkulic's father-in-law, John Morgan, purchased an old stainless-steel diner car, which was operating as the Dutch Kitchen, and moved it fifty miles from its original location in Allentown, Pennsylvania, to Frackville. Morgan kept the original name when he reopened it, and added a sit-down restaurant to the diner car in 1972.

Locals are quick to tell you that no Pennsylvania Dutch dinner is complete without a slice of shoofly pie. Some believe the name of the pie came from bakers having to shoo away flies drawn to the sweet, sticky pools of molasses that formed on top, while others claim that shoofly is a corruption of the French word for cauliflower (*chou-fleur*), as the crumbly top slightly resembles the vegetable. Whichever the correct origin may be, this thick, gooey pie is served in both wet- and dry-bottom varieties, and both are baked fresh daily at the Dutch Kitchen.

The Dutch Kitchen's wet-bottom pie recipe came from Mrs. Weir, a wonderful baker and old neighbor of Levkulic's, and was only recently added to the menu. A word of caution, though, to the uninitiated: Shoofly pie is unlike anything you've ever made before. "When you make it, it literally has the consistency of water," Levkulic says. "You just ladle it into the pie shell. It bakes and forms a gooey jelly on the bottom. It bakes from the top down, and there's just enough flour to stop it from cooking right on the bottom. You make it and think, 'Oh, what did I forget?'"

Wet-Bottom Shoofly Pie

Filling

    1 cup all-purpose flour

    $3/4$ cup packed brown sugar

    1 tablespoon margarine, at room temperature

    1 cup molasses

    1 egg, beaten

    $3/4$ cup boiling water

    $1\frac{1}{4}$ teaspoons baking soda

    1 teaspoon hot water

1 partially baked 10-inch pie shell (page 8)

Preheat the oven to 375°F. In a large bowl, mix together the flour, brown sugar, and margarine by hand. Set aside $1/2$ cup of the mixture for the crumb topping. In a separate bowl, mix together the molasses, egg, and boiling water. Dissolve the baking soda in the 1 teaspoon hot water, then add to the molasses mixture. Pour the molasses mixture into the flour mixture and mix well; pour into the pie shell. (You might have some filling left over.) Sprinkle the reserved crumb topping on the pie.

Bake for 20 minutes, then turn the temperature down to 350°F and bake for an additional 20 minutes. The topping should be golden and the bottom should be gooey. *Makes one 10-inch single-crust pie.*

GENERAL BAKIN' TIPS

★ Before it's baked, the filling should have the consistency of water. Traditional doneness-testing methods, such as sticking a toothpick through the middle, don't work with shoofly pie because it tastes best when gooey.

★ Follow the baking times to ensure a properly baked pie. More or less time, or a slightly higher or lower oven temperature, will affect the pie's unique wet bottom.

PONZIO'S

CHERRY HILL, NEW JERSEY

In the late 1940s, Jim Ponzio decided to open a restaurant in southern New Jersey that would provide his customers with delicious homemade food and the very latest in comfort and sanitation: air-conditioning and an automatic dishwasher. Since then, Ponzio's has changed ownership and locations, but the ardent attention to their customers hasn't changed a bit. The current owners, the Fifis family—father Jim, brothers John, Nick, and Chris, and cousin John Giambanis—bought Ponzio's in 1958 and expanded it into a large family-dining establishment, complete with six dining rooms, a cocktail lounge, and a takeout counter. The restaurant also boasts an ample retail bakery, which features 130 different kinds of baked goods, including cheesecakes, rugelach, cookies, hamentashen, cheese rolls, and pies.

One of Ponzio's exceptionally popular items is their mouthwatering pumpkin pie. Instead of baking with standard canned pumpkin, they use the pulp of fresh pumpkins, grown especially for them by nearby Springdale Farms. Using fresh pumpkin is certainly more labor-intensive, but it's a labor of love they have no problem providing for their many devoted customers. John Fifis thinks this extra effort is the secret to the restaurant's success: "We have stayed in business for over forty years because of our hands-on approach, making sure our customers receive great service and great food."

Ponzio's Pumpkin Pie

Filling

   One 3- to 5-pound pie pumpkin

   10 tablespoons sugar

   $\frac{1}{4}$ cup nonfat dry milk

   $\frac{1}{2}$ cup corn syrup

   $\frac{1}{4}$ teaspoon ground cinnamon

   $\frac{1}{4}$ teaspoon ground cloves

   $\frac{1}{4}$ teaspoon ground ginger

   $\frac{1}{4}$ teaspoon salt

   $\frac{1}{2}$ cup heavy cream

   2 eggs, beaten

   $1\frac{1}{4}$ cups milk

1 partially baked 9-inch pie shell (page 8)

Cut the skin off the pumpkin, cut it in half, and clean out the strings and seeds. Place the pumpkin in a kettle of boiling water and boil until tender. Carefully remove the pumpkin and place in a cheesecloth square, tying it up as tightly as possible. Hang overnight over a pan or bowl to collect the draining juices. Or, line a colander with cheesecloth, coffee filters, or a thin, clean dishtowel, set the colander on top of a bowl, and place the boiled pumpkin in the colander. Cover with plastic wrap and let stand overnight.

Remove the pumpkin from the cheesecloth or colander and puree in a food processor. Preheat the oven to 375°F. In a large bowl, combine the pumpkin, sugar, dry milk, corn syrup, spices, and salt. In a separate bowl, combine the cream, eggs, and milk, then add to the pumpkin mixture. Pour into the pie crust and bake for 1 hour and 10 minutes to 20 minutes, or until set. Allow the pie to cool before serving. *Makes one 9-inch single-crust pie.*

GENERAL BAKIN' TIP

★ Ponzio's uses the water remaining in the kettle after boiling a pumpkin as stock for pumpkin soup.

MIDWESTERN U.S. · KILLER PIES

SWEETIE PIES

── FISH CREEK, WISCONSIN ──

Wisconsin's Door County is frequently referred to as "Cherryland, USA," so it makes sense that this cheerful fruit would fill the most popular kind of pie from Door County bakery Sweetie Pies. A busy tourist spot, the county extends across part of a peninsula that juts into Green Bay and Lake Michigan, and the quaint village of Fish Creek is situated on bluffs that overlook the water. Visitors often call it the Cape Cod of the Midwest.

Capitalizing on the bounty of lush local fruit, Fish Creek resident Susan Croissant—perhaps the most appropriately named baker in history—opened Sweetie Pies in 1995, and baked pies using recipes from her grandmother. Eight years later, Croissant married and moved away, and Sweetie Pies employee Corinne Lea and her father, David, decided to buy the pie shop. "We couldn't imagine the pie shop closing down," David says. "We just said, 'Well, why not?'" The Leas inherited many of Croissant's recipes, and with the help of a small team of five bakers, they bake two hundred pies each day, including apple-caramel-walnut, lemon meringue, and the renowned cherry. The tart Montmorency cherries grown locally in Door County are sometimes called sour, red, or pie cherries; other varieties, such as Early Richmond and Morello, will also work well in Sweetie Pies' bona fide recipe.

Door County Cherry Pie

Crust

> $1/3$ cup cold salted butter
>
> $1/2$ cup vegetable shortening
>
> 2 rounded cups unbleached all-purpose flour
>
> About $1/2$ cup cold water

Preheat the oven to 325°F. Use a food processor to cut the butter and shortening into the flour to form pea-sized lumps. Place the mixture in a large bowl. Add enough water to hold the dough together, incorporate it roughly with your hands, and squeeze the mixture hard to form a ball of dough. (Do not overmix or overwork the dough at this point; work quickly.) Cut the dough into quarters and roll out each piece into a round shape about $1/8$ inch thick and 11 inches in diameter to make 4 pastry rounds. Fit bottom crusts into two 9-inch pie pans and trim the edges.

Filling

> $1/2$ cup all-purpose flour
>
> 1 cup sugar
>
> 8 cups fresh tart pie cherries, pitted
>
> 2 tablespoons unsalted butter, cut into small pieces

Milk, for brushing

Sugar, for sprinkling

Mix the flour and sugar in a bowl. Spread $1/4$ cup onto the bottom of 1 pie crust. Spread 2 cups cherries evenly over the flour-sugar mixture and sprinkle half of the pieces of butter on them. Sprinkle another $1/3$ cup of the flour-sugar mixture evenly over the cherries. Gently spread another 2 cups of cherries on top. Place a top crust over the cherries and seal the edge of the pie by folding the top crust under the bottom crust and pushing lightly to the edge of the pie tin. Repeat for the second pie. Brush milk evenly over the top of each pie with a pastry brush. Sprinkle sugar on top and cut a few slits on the top of the pie to allow steam to escape. Bake the pies for 1 to $1^1/2$ hours, until the top is golden and the juice is shiny. Cool at least 1 to 2 hours before cutting. *Makes two 9-inch double-crust pies.*

CHEYENNE RIDGE OUTFITTERS & LODGE

PIERRE, SOUTH DAKOTA

Cheyenne Ridge, in the South Dakota capital of Pierre, is neither a bakery nor a restaurant; it's a hunting lodge. It has the requisite mounted taxidermy, and it also has fantastic food, courtesy of JoAnne Oaks. The talented chef has a close connection to the land surrounding her workplace, as her family has been living and farming in South Dakota since 1870—and Oaks has proof: "I have photos of my family in covered wagons going to pick fruit at the river." Back then, of course, frontier families living on the Plains lacked the luxury of grocery stores full of produce from all over the world. "They didn't have apples and oranges," she says. "They gleaned from the land the things they could, like wild plums and chokecherries growing along the Missouri River."

Now, groups coming to Cheyenne Ridge to hunt pheasant and other types of fowl—the lodge is located on a pheasant preserve—can taste some of South Dakota's history in the food that Oaks makes. Many of her recipes have been passed down through generations, including the one for sour cream plum pie. Her family has been baking this pie for more than 100 years, and it's become a holiday tradition. "I'm one of nine children, and none of us would think it was Christmas without this pie," she says. "We just have to have it."

Sour Cream Plum Pie

Filling

- 1 quart canned wild plums
- 1¼ cups sugar
- 2 tablespoons all-purpose flour
- 1 cup sour cream

Preheat the oven to 350°F. Drain and pit plums. Mix together the sugar and flour in a bowl, then fold in the sour cream and plums.

Double-crust pie dough (page 8)
Milk, for brushing
Sugar and cinnamon to taste, for sprinkling

On a lightly floured board, roll each disk of dough into an 11-inch round. Fit 1 round of the dough into a 9-inch pie pan. Add the filling. Cover with the top crust, flute edges, and brush with milk and sprinkle with sugar and cinnamon. Cut vents in the crust and bake for 1 hour. *Makes one 9-inch double-crust pie.*

GENERAL BAKIN' TIP

★ Oaks uses wild plums that are grown in South Dakota and then canned, but there are many different varieties of plums that grow all over North America. If you can't find canned plums, choose fresh ones that are in season. Visit farmers' markets and orchards, where you can ask the grower firsthand what he or she recommends. Or, better yet, keep experimenting until you find your favorite.

STAGECOACH INN BED & BREAKFAST

CEDARBURG, WISCONSIN

The Stagecoach Inn touts itself as "a little country inn in the city," and visitors enjoy the best of both worlds: comfort and a bit of history (it's within walking distance to Cedar Creek Settlement), a covey of shops, art galleries, restaurants, a winery, and various annual festivals, all in downtown Cedarburg. The historic inn was built in 1853 and once served as a hotel for travelers making the trip by stagecoach between Green Bay and Milwaukee. Nowadays, Cedarburg residents and visitors can hop in the car and find themselves in Milwaukee just twenty minutes later.

There's plenty to do in Cedarburg and beyond, but most guests are just as content to stay in while they're quartered at the cozy B&B. Owners Brook and Liz Brown refurbished the Greek Revival building in the mid-1980s to include comfy guest rooms, a pub, and—perhaps most essential—a chocolate shop. Visitors may also opt to stay in one of the three rooms in Weber Haus, the inn's annex across the street. All rooms in both buildings are decorated with antiques—Cedarburg is known by many as the antiques capital of Wisconsin. Plus, lovers of nature can relax in the Weber Haus' private, lush perennial garden. If all that fails to captivate guests, the aroma of Liz Brown's apple pie will keep them lingering. Her recipe features a crunchy walnut topping to complement the sweet, moist apple filling.

Sweet Apple Pie

Filling

> 1 cup sugar
>
> 1 cup sour cream
>
> 1/2 cup all-purpose flour
>
> 1 egg
>
> 2 teaspoons vanilla extract
>
> 8 Granny Smith or other tart apples, peeled, cored, and sliced

1 unbaked 9-inch deep-dish pie shell (page 8); see tip

Preheat the oven to 400°F. Blend the sugar, sour cream, flour, egg, and vanilla extract until smooth. Mix in the apples and pour filling into the pie shell. Bake the pie for 45 minutes.

Topping

> 1/2 cup (1 stick) unsalted butter
>
> 1 1/2 cups chopped walnut pieces
>
> 1/2 cup sugar
>
> 3/4 cup all-purpose flour
>
> 1 tablespoon ground cinnamon
>
> 1/2 cup packed brown sugar

Mix all ingredients together. Sprinkle evenly over the baked pie and bake for 5 additional minutes. *Makes one 9-inch single-crust pie.*

GENERAL BAKIN' TIP

★ For a deep-dish pie, roll out the disk of dough into a 14-inch round.

LANGE'S CAFÉ

PIPESTONE, MINNESOTA

In 1956, twin brothers Roy and Les Lange opened Lange's Café in Pipestone, Minnesota, and pledged to stay open twenty-four hours a day, 365 days a year. They felt so strongly about this that they buried the keys to the café in cement. Fifty years later, the Lange promise still holds true; the café has never once closed its doors. Les's son Steve is committed to keeping his father and uncle's dream alive, so much so that the café no longer has locks on the doors.

The café's slogan, "Where Old Friends Meet," couldn't be more sincere. In Pipestone, a small town in southwestern Minnesota with a population of about five thousand, when friends want to meet, chances are they'll do their meeting at Lange's. The place exudes cheerful friendliness and hospitality, as well as great fill-you-up homemade food—the breakfast menu alone is six pages long. For dessert, diners can savor pies, cinnamon and caramel rolls, and ice cream, all delectable, homemade treats. Lange's makes thirty varieties of pies, but number one in the hearts of its loyal customers is the sour cream raisin, a Midwestern specialty. The pie doesn't have the beauty of, say, a sunny lemon meringue or lattice-top blueberry pie, but what it lacks in looks, it certainly makes up for in taste.

Sour Cream Raisin Pie

Crust

$1/4$ cup pastry flour

$1/2$ cup all-purpose flour

$1/8$ teaspoon baking powder

$1/3$ teaspoon salt

$1/3$ cup lard

1 egg, beaten (only $1/3$ of egg will be used)

$3/4$ teaspoon distilled white vinegar

$1 1/4$ tablespoons water

Preheat the oven to 350°F. Mix together the flours, baking powder, and salt. Add the lard and mix by hand until crumbly and small beads form. Mix together one-third of the egg, vinegar, and water in a separate bowl. Add to the flour mixture and mix well with your hands. Roll the dough out to an 11-inch round and fit into a 9-inch pie pan. Flute the edges and prick the dough with a fork. Bake for 15 minutes. Press out any air bubbles and let cool.

Filling

4 cups raisins

1 cup cornstarch

12 egg yolks

5 cups packed brown sugar

4 cups sour cream

Put the raisins in a saucepan and add just enough water to cover them. Boil until the raisins absorb the water. Mix together the remaining ingredients. Add to the raisins and cook, stirring from the bottom, until thick. Pour into the pie crust.

Meringue

$3/4$ cup egg whites (about 6)

1 teaspoon cream of tartar

$1/4$ cup superfine sugar

Whip the egg whites and cream of tartar at high speed. When the mixture begins to thicken, add the sugar. Continue beating at high speed for another 2 minutes. Mound the meringue on top of the filled pie and lift into peaks, making sure all the filling is covered. Bake for about 17 minutes, or until lightly brown. *Makes one 9-inch single-crust pie.*

AROUND THE CLOCK RESTAURANT & BAKERY

CRYSTAL LAKE, ILLINOIS

Fans of Around the Clock Restaurant & Bakery eat breakfast, lunch, dinner, and dessert at all hours at this inviting establishment. Owner Steve Theofanous estimates the restaurant serves ten thousand people each week—a hugely impressive number that proves just how popular this spot is.

In the diner's full-service bakery, pies are made from scratch by Noreen Sye, the resident "pie specialist," and her crew. Many of Sye's pies, including the cherry, blushing peach, and apple varieties, have won blue ribbons at the local McHenry County Fair. Other favorites include berry, coconut, and banana, plus seasonal delights like cranberry apple and strawberry rhubarb. Folks in the know commonly say that a meal at the restaurant isn't complete without dessert, and people take that mantra very seriously, ordering cake, pie, and other pastries by the boatload. Thanksgiving is the busiest time for the bakery, when they sell an astounding one thousand pies! And during the rest of year, the apple pies alone require the peeling, coring, and slicing of two hundred apples each day.

Apple Pie

Crust

> 6 cups all-purpose flour
>
> 3 tablespoons salt
>
> 2 $\frac{2}{3}$ cups vegetable shortening
>
> 2 eggs, beaten
>
> 4 tablespoons distilled white vinegar
>
> 7 tablespoons water

Mix together the flour and salt. Add the shortening and mix with your fingers to form a crumblike consistency. Mix the eggs and vinegar with water in a separate bowl, then add the liquid mixture to the dough. Mix lightly with your hand in a clawlike motion, but don't overwork; the dough should barely hold together. Form into a ball and divide into 6 equal parts.

Filling

> 7 cups Granny Smith apples, peeled, cored, and sliced
>
> 1 cup sugar
>
> $\frac{1}{8}$ teaspoon ground nutmeg
>
> 1 teaspoon ground cinnamon
>
> 1 teaspoon tapioca flour
>
> 1 $\frac{1}{2}$ tablespoons unsalted butter, cut into small pieces

Preheat the oven to 325°F. Combine the first 5 ingredients in a large mixing bowl and toss until the apples are evenly coated. On a lightly floured board, roll out one part of the dough into an 11-inch round. Fit into a 9-inch pie pan, leaving 1 inch of dough hanging over the edge of the pan. Fill the crust with the apple mixture (you may have some left over) and dot with butter. Roll out another part of the dough for the top crust. Cut five 2-inch slits all around the center and place on top of the pie. Pinch the overhanging dough together, roll under, and crimp with your thumb and forefinger to seal around the edge. Place the pie on a small baking sheet to catch dripping juices.

Bake the pie for 55 minutes, or until the filling is bubbly and the crust is golden. *Makes one 9-inch double-crust pie, plus dough for two more double-crust pies.*

DEERFIELD'S BAKERY

DEERFIELD, ILLINOIS

Like many immigrants, when the Schmitt family moved to Chicago from Wiesloch, Germany, in the late 1800s, they brought with them recipes from their homeland. Patriarch Adam Schmitt put these recipes to use and opened his own bakery and deli soon after their arrival. After serving in World War II, Adam's son Henry returned to Chicago and expanded the family business, eventually opening nearly forty Schmitt Bake Shops throughout the city and surrounding suburbs. After filing for bankruptcy, however, Henry Schmitt scaled back his business. He decided to concentrate his efforts on a location in Deerfield, Illinois, with the help of his children, Kurt, Kathi, and Karl, who left their respective careers to join the family business. The bakery was renamed Deerfield's, in honor of its new home, and blossomed into a more urban and upscale affair, leaving behind its Old World style. The bakery is also self-serve, where patrons peruse the varieties of baked items set out for sale and choose their own.

The family has since opened two more Deerfield's locations in Illinois, in Buffalo Grove and in Schaumburg, the latter of which is housed in a Tudor-style building that harkens back to the family's European roots. The mouthwatering baked goods recall the Schmitts' ancestry, too. Customers can purchase Hungarian strudel, fruitcakes, challah, and holiday stollen—all made from family recipes. Deerfield's is perhaps best known in the Chicago area for its elaborately decorated cakes, and the bakery has collected numerous decorating honors and was named National Retail Bakery of the Year by *Bakery* magazine, a mark of pride reflected in their pecan pie.

Pecan Pie

3 tablespoons honey

½ cup corn syrup

¼ cup (½ stick) unsalted butter

10 tablespoons packed brown sugar

2 eggs

1 teaspoon vanilla extract

1 unbaked 9-inch pie shell (page 8)

½ cup pecan halves

Preheat the oven to 350°F. Mix together the honey, corn syrup, butter, and brown sugar and heat in a saucepan until the sugar dissolves. Let the mixture cool. Beat the eggs and vanilla together and stir into the sugar mixture. Line the pie shell with the pecan halves (which will rise to the top while the pie is baking) and pour the filling on top. Bake for 1 hour, and allow the pie to cool before serving. *Makes one 9-inch single-crust pie.*

GENERAL BAKIN' TIP

★ Eggs work as a binding agent in pie fillings. But if they're added to hot liquid, they will scramble, so be sure the sugar mixture is cool before adding the eggs.

MIDWESTERN U.S.

KILLER PIES

STONE'S RESTAURANT

MARSHALLTOWN, IOWA

Esbon Weed Stone was born in Marshalltown, after his parents moved there from Canada in a covered wagon in 1850. In 1887, he opened Stone's Restaurant to cater to weary railroad passengers and crews passing through Marshalltown, and the place has been an Iowa staple ever since. In 1910, the restaurant moved into an old hotel-tavern-billiards hall under the original 3rd Avenue viaduct in Marshalltown. The directions to this address, "under the viaduct, down by the vinegar works," stuck and became the eatery's tag line. Though several generations of Stones have run Stone's, the slogan remains to this day, and is even printed on the placemats.

What has also survived—and is printed on the placemats—is the recipe for the famous "Mile-High" Lemon Chiffon Pie. Developed by Anna Stone, the wife of Esbon's son George, in the 1930s, the pie and the rest of the restaurant's food draws attention from across the country. *Life*, *The Saturday Evening Post*, and *National Geographic* have published stories about the eatery, and Duncan Hines, the renowned travel guide writer, cookbook author, and food company namesake, reportedly claimed he'd travel 100 miles out of his way to eat at Stone's. Customers dine on hand-cut chops and steaks, fried chicken, roast beef, and other down-home comfort foods. But it's the pie that has really kept Stone's in the spotlight. The gravity-defying lemon chiffon pie is so airy and light, it practically floats above the plate.

"Mile-High" Lemon Chiffon Pie

Filling

>**8 eggs, separated**
>**2 cups sugar**
>**Juice of 2 lemons**
>**Grated zest of 2 lemons**
>**Salt, to taste**
>**2 envelopes unflavored gelatin**
>**1/2 cup cold water**

1 fully baked 9-inch pie shell (page 8)
Whipped cream

Lightly beat the egg yolks. Combine the yolks, 1 cup of the sugar, the lemon juice, grated lemon zest, and salt in a double boiler. Cook over barely simmering water, stirring frequently, until the mixture reaches the consistency of a thick custard. Remove from the heat. Soak the gelatin in the cold water until dissolved, then stir into to the hot custard. Let cool.

Beat the egg whites until stiff, but not dry. Beat in the remaining 1 cup sugar gradually, mixing well. Fold the cooled custard into the beaten egg whites. Pour the filling into the pie crust and chill for 3 hours. Serve with whipped cream. *Makes one 9-inch single-crust pie.*

MIDWESTERN U.S. ★ ★ KILLER PIES

JOHNNY'S CAFÉ

— OMAHA, NEBRASKA —

It seems appropriate that Johnny's Café—"Omaha's original steakhouse"—is located next to what once were the largest stockyards in the United States. Since 1922, the café has been providing Nebraskans with steaks that are hand-cut and aged on the premises, slow-roasted prime rib, braised ox tails, chicken and dumplings, and other meaty morsels.

The Kawa family has owned and operated Johnny's for three generations. Patriarch Frank Kawa, a Polish immigrant, turned a saloon with a handful of seats into a thriving Omaha landmark, and now Frank's granddaughters, Sally and Kari, run the business. Johnny's

has maintained a traditional steakhouse feel over the years, with oversized red leather chairs and booths—plenty of room to loosen your belt and devour a chateaubriand or T-bone in comfort. And speaking of T-bones, don't forget to check out the ceiling. The beams that run the length of the main dining room and the bar are shaped like the choice loin steak.

After diners finish their delicious suppers, they'll more than likely follow with dessert, whether they've saved room or not. According to Sally Kawa, one of the café's most popular desserts is the decadent pecan pie, which is baked daily on site.

Johnny's Café Pecan Pie

Filling

$\frac{1}{4}$ cup ($\frac{1}{2}$ stick) unsalted butter, melted

2 cups light corn syrup

3 cups plus 6 tablespoons sugar

1 tablespoon salt

12 eggs

1 tablespoon vanilla extract

$\frac{3}{4}$ cup small pecan pieces

1 unbaked 9-inch pie shell (page 8)

Preheat the oven to 350°F. Combine all the filling ingredients except the pecans and mix well. Sprinkle the pecans in the bottom of the pie shell, and pour the filling on top. Bake for 50 to 60 minutes, until golden brown. Allow to cool before slicing. *Makes one 9-inch single-crust pie.*

JUST PIES

WORTHINGTON, OHIO

When bakers Peter Sterk and Vicki Stevens opened their Ohio bakery in 1995, they wanted to be sure the name made obvious what they were selling. Luckily, the name, as well as their amazing pies, have attracted quite a bit of attention in the more than ten years since Just Pies first opened its doors. In fact, they've been honored on two notable "best of" lists: the 2003 "Only the Best" episode of *Oprah* and the Food Network's program *The Best Of*. Just Pies has also expanded, and there are now two locations in the Columbus area—the original storefront in Worthington, and a new retail shop/bakery in Westerville.

Not only are the pies delicious, there are plenty of them. The more than forty different varieties include basics such as cherry, peach, and banana cream, as well as specialty pies, such as pecan chocolate-chip cookie and pineapple, while those watching their sugar intake can choose from seven no-sugar-added pies. The buckeye cream, which they create by whipping peanut butter into their rich, chocolate-laden French silk pie, is a regional favorite, too. All of Just Pies' pies are made from scratch, but manager Brian Wilhelms understands that even with the best intentions, we sometimes need to save time in the kitchen. This tasty version of the bakery's chocolate-covered cherry pie uses quick and easy ingredients, such as Nestlé's Choco Bake, a pre-melted chocolate that eliminates the hassle of melting your own. Pie purists, of course, are free to make pie crusts from scratch, melt their own chocolate, and make fresh whipped cream.

Chocolate-Covered Cherry Pie

Filling

$^3/_4$ cup (1$^1/_2$ sticks) unsalted butter, at room temperature

1$^1/_2$ cups sugar

2 teaspoons vanilla extract

Four 1-ounce packages Nestlé's Choco Bake unsweetened chocolate

3 large eggs

1 cup prepared cherry pie filling

1 fully baked 9-inch pie shell (page 8)

1 cup Cool Whip

Chocolate for drizzling, such as Hershey's Magic Shell

1 maraschino cherry

Beat the butter, sugar, and vanilla until light and fluffy. Add the chocolate and mix with an electric mixer on medium speed for about 1 minute, scraping the bowl as you go to blend well. Add the eggs one at a time, beating the mixture for 3 minutes after each egg.

Spread a shallow layer of the chocolate mixture in the pie crust. Pour the cherry pie filling on top. Add the remaining chocolate mixture, filling to the top of the pie shell. Chill the pie for 3 hours. Top with Cool Whip, chocolate drizzle, and the cherry. *Makes one 9-inch single-crust pie.*

GENERAL BAKIN' TIP

★ For a richer pie, use a prebaked graham-cracker crust.

THE GOLDEN LAMB

LEBANON, OHIO

Like the Stagecoach Inn in Wisconsin (page 34), the Golden Lamb historically was a respite for stagecoach travelers who needed to stretch their legs and fill their bellies. Established in 1803, the Golden Lamb is Ohio's oldest hotel, and through the years it has been visited by the likes of Charles Dickens, Mark Twain, and a dozen U.S. presidents, from James Garfield to George W. Bush.

Even today, patrons don't have to struggle much to envision what life was like back in the olden days. Despite some modern additions, the Golden Lamb has mostly maintained its old-time look, feel, and charm. The menu contains traditional hearty fare such as trout, duckling, family-style servings of fried chicken and roast beef, and, of course, roasted lamb. Waitresses wear gingham uniforms, and the dining rooms are decorated in Victorian-era antiques and paintings.

Though the Golden Lamb's lemon pie tends to get the most acclaim, its Shaker sugar pie best captures the inn's long history, as well as Ohio's roots as a settlement for Shakers, an offshoot of the Quakers. Much like a Southern chess pie, the sugar pie is a "staple" pie, made with ingredients found in every kitchen— butter, flour, cream, brown sugar. And also like chess pie, this pie's sweetness is best complemented by a cup of strong black coffee or tea while chowing down.

Sister Lizzie's Shaker Sugar Pie

$\frac{1}{3}$ cup all-purpose flour

1 cup packed brown sugar

1 unbaked 9-inch pie shell (page 8)

2 cups light cream

1 teaspoon vanilla extract

2 tablespoons unsalted butter, sliced into pieces

Grated nutmeg, for sprinkling

Preheat the oven to 350°F. Thoroughly mix together the flour and brown sugar and spread evenly in the bottom of the pie shell. Mix together the cream and vanilla. Pour the cream mixture into the shell. Distribute the sliced butter evenly on top. Sprinkle with nutmeg. Bake for 40 to 45 minutes, or until firm. *Makes one 9-inch single-crust pie.*

THE HAM SHOPPE

VALLE CRUCIS, NORTH CAROLINA

Nestled in the bosky Blue Ridge Mountains of western North Carolina, the Ham Shoppe is a full-service store that offers tourists and locals alike a chance to meet and greet, pick up groceries, and eat. Not surprisingly, the Ham Shoppe's main specialty is ham, particularly country hams. Customers can also treat themselves to made-from-scratch Southern favorites, such as biscuits, grits, breads, and delicious pies, baked each day by Ham Shoppe baker Sharon Potter.

Valle Crucis, which means "vale of the cross" in Latin, is small and rural, though the influx of tourists trekking to the state's verdant mountains has increased substantially in recent years. Though technically a country store, the Ham Shoppe is no slow-as-molasses operation; it is nearly always busy and bustling,

even more so when car-racing fans flock to the Bristol Speedway, about sixty miles away.

One of Potter's best pies is her strawberry-rhubarb pie. She gets her rhubarb already cleaned and diced from a local grower, but you can purchase the thick stalks in markets and grocery stores and prepare them at home. Rhubarb has maintained its status as a popular pie ingredient for centuries—so much so that German speakers frequently refer to it as *piestengel*, or "pie plant." It resembles red celery, and it's far too tart to eat raw, but rhubarb cooks and bakes beautifully when combined with sweeter ingredients, adding a bit of bite to pies, jams, compotes, and even wine. Of this pie Potter says, "This is as good as it gets. The color is lovely, the taste divine, and it's just tart enough to surprise you."

Strawberry-Rhubarb Pie

Filling

> 1 pound rhubarb
>
> 1 cup sugar
>
> 5 tablespoons all-purpose flour
>
> 1 pint fresh strawberries

Preheat the oven to 350°F. Wash the rhubarb, trim ends, and cut into ¾-inch chunks. Place in a bowl with the sugar and flour, mix together well, and set aside. Wash and hull the strawberries and slice them in half or quarters, depending on their size. By now, the sugar and flour should have softened the rhubarb; if not, wait 5 more minutes. Add the strawberries to the rhubarb mixture and gently mix.

Double-crust pie dough (page 8)
2 tablespoons unsalted butter
¼ teaspoon freshly grated nutmeg

Divide the pie dough in half. On a lightly floured board, roll each half into an 11-inch round. Fit 1 round of pastry into a 9-inch pie pan. Spoon the fruit mixture into the pie crust, dot with the butter, and sprinkle on the nutmeg. Place the top crust over the pie and seal by fluting the edges. Bake for 1 hour, or until the crust is lightly browned and the juices bubble up. Cool completely on a wire rack before cutting. *Makes one 9-inch double-crust pie.*

GENERAL BAKIN' TIP

★ Rhubarb can be frozen in plastic freezer bags for up to a year. If you're using frozen rhubarb, be sure to remove all excess water beforehand. Sharon Potter recommends pressing out moisture rather than just draining it. Rhubarb is 95 percent water already, and the added moisture from the freezing process increases this amount, resulting in a soggy pie. Fresh rhubarb, however, does not need to be drained. And always avoid the leaves; they are toxic.

DANGEROUSLY DELICIOUS PIES

BALTIMORE, MARYLAND

Rock 'n' roll and pie generally don't beg a comparison. Pies are more Aunt Lizzy than Thin Lizzy, and when we think of hands gently rolling out dough and slicing fruit, we don't imagine those hands attached to tattoo-covered arms. But once upon a time, a young boy named Rodney Henry baked a Bob Andy pie with his grandma. When he grew older, Henry temporarily traded his rolling pin for rockin' out, moved east to Baltimore, and started a band. Finding himself broke after a tour with his band, he decided to make money by baking a few pies to sell to local coffee shops. Soon he was baking so often that he decided to start his own business, and in 2003, Dangerously Delicious Pies was born. "That's when I became legitimate," Henry says.

Dangerously Delicious Pies is simultaneously nothing and everything you'd expect: The shop's logo, for instance, is a pie and crossbones. Henry describes DDP as a "pie dive" and a "honky-tonk pie shop," where people can eat pie and listen to live music a few nights a week. The décor is retro kitsch—more James Dean than Doris Day—and the butter-and-lard crusts melt in your mouth. The Bob Andy pie is "a really awesome pie," Henry says. "I call it 'White Trash Crème Brûlée.'" The pie is considered a "staple" pie, meaning it contains the basic ingredients most people have in their cupboards at any given moment.

Bob Andy Pie

Filling

> 3 eggs, separated
>
> 2 cups sugar
>
> 1 tablespoon ground cinnamon
>
> 3 tablespoons all-purpose flour
>
> 1 cup unsalted butter, melted
>
> 3 scant cups milk

1 unbaked 9-inch pie shell (page 8)

Preheat the oven to 375°F. Mix all the filling ingredients, except the egg whites, together to make a custard. With a hand mixer, beat the whites in a separate bowl until stiff peaks form, about 5 minutes. Fold the whites into the custard and pour into the pie shell. Bake for 1 hour. *Makes one 9-inch single-crust pie.*

GENERAL BAKIN' TIPS

★ Rodney Henry says that the pie is done when "everything moves together. It shouldn't be jiggly like milk."

★ Cold eggs are easiest to separate. Then, let the egg whites stand at room temperature for 30 minutes, or microwave them for about 20 seconds, taking care not to let them cook. Using room-temperature eggs for your meringue will achieve better volume.

McEWEN'S ON MONROE

MEMPHIS, TENNESSEE

While Southern foods such as gumbo, grits, and biscuits and gravy get far more culinary attention, few desserts whistle Dixie quite like banana cream pie. In other parts of the United States, however, banana cream pie suffers a low-brow reputation in fine-dining establishments. Some consider it too denture-friendly, too simple, too diner-y—not that there's anything wrong with any of those things. Luckily, McEwen's on Monroe's more sophisticated version of the pie forces naysayers to banish such thoughts.

McEwen's on Monroe, named for owners Mac and Cathy Edwards' niece, Frances McEwen Edwards, opened its doors in 1997, and has evolved into one of Memphis's most popular dining spots. Food critics dubbed the McEwen's fare "Southern fusion," but patrons care less about the label and more that the food is just really, really good. Edwards prides himself on the fact that diners will "never have to go home and eat a bowl of cereal after they've eaten here." And much of the restaurant's success is due, at least in part, to the creamy, delectable banana cream pie. The banana added to the traditional graham-cracker crust intensifies the flavor and makes the crust enticingly chewy.

Banana Cream Pie

Crust

    2$\frac{1}{2}$ cups graham cracker crumbs

    $\frac{1}{3}$ cup sugar

    1 very ripe, slightly brown banana, peeled and mashed

    $\frac{1}{4}$ cup ($\frac{1}{2}$ stick) unsalted butter, melted

Mix all the ingredients in a large mixing bowl. Press into the bottom and up the sides of a 10-inch pie pan. Chill until firm, about 30 minutes. Preheat the oven to 350°F. Bake the crust for about 15 minutes, until lightly golden. Cool completely.

Filling

    3 cups heavy cream

    2 tablespoons water

    $\frac{1}{3}$ cup cornstarch

    $\frac{1}{4}$ teaspoon salt

    3 egg yolks

    $\frac{1}{2}$ cup sugar

    2 tablespoons unsalted butter, melted

    1$\frac{1}{2}$ teaspoons vanilla extract

    $\frac{1}{2}$ vanilla bean, split lengthwise

    3 slightly ripened bananas, peeled and sliced $\frac{1}{4}$ inch thick

Chocolate and caramel, for drizzling

Add the first 8 ingredients to a saucepan. Scrape the seeds from the vanilla bean into the pan, then add the bean. Cook over medium-high heat until the mixture boils, whisking constantly until the mixture thickens. Remove the vanilla bean. Reduce the heat to low and cook 1 minute. Set aside to cool completely, whisking occasionally, for about 1 hour.

Smooth 1 cup of filling in the bottom of the prepared crust. Layer 1 banana on the filling. Add another cup of filling and layer another banana, and repeat the process one more time, so the filling reaches just above the shell. Chill the pie until the filling is set, at least 8 hours and up to 1 day. Drizzle chocolate and caramel on top. *Makes one 10-inch single-crust pie.*

THE MORRISON-CLARK INN

WASHINGTON, DISTRICT OF COLUMBIA

The nation's capital is chock-full of historic sites, and the Morrison-Clark Inn is no exception. In 1864, developer David Morrison and land investor Reuben Clark, both wealthy men, each built ritzy Victorian-style town homes at Massachusetts Avenue and Eleventh Street. In 1987, under the watchful eye of renowned renovation supervisor William Adair, the two homes merged to become the Morrison-Clark Inn.

Adair ensured that the inn retained the charm, history, and décor of its illustrious past. The expansive Chinese Chippendale porch, with its terracotta-hued Shanghai roof, remains, as does the rest of the old exterior architecture. Inside, guests will find fireplaces made of Italian Carrara marble and rooms decorated with period furniture and antiques.

Visitors will also find an award-winning restaurant.

Pennsylvania native Craig Hartman became the Inn's executive chef in 2005 and maintains its reputation for some of the District of Columbia's finest food. Though he's racked up accolade after accolade, the chef unabashedly says that he became a cook because he simply loves food and loves to eat. In particular, Hartman loves Southern food and fresh seafood, which remind him of boyhood summers spent at his family's hotel in Ocean City, Maryland. Every self-respecting Southerner (or admirer of Southern cuisine) knows to save room for a slice of chess pie and a cup of coffee at the end of a meal, and the Inn doesn't let guests down: Hartman and his team serve a kicked-up version of the old standby—a lemon-flavored chess pie with a coconut crust, which you can garnish with a fresh blackberry compote if you like.

Lemon Chess Pie

Crust

- $3/4$ cup all-purpose flour
- $1/3$ cup unsweetened shredded coconut
- 1 teaspoon sugar
- $1/8$ teaspoon salt
- 10 tablespoons cold unsalted butter, cut into pieces
- $2^1/2$ tablespoons ice water

Preheat the oven to 350°F. Combine the flour, coconut, sugar, and salt in a food processor and pulse several times to mix. Add the butter and pulse until most of the mixture resembles coarse meal, with some pieces in pea-sized lumps. Add the water and pulse just until the mixture forms a dough. (Do not overmix or the pastry will be tough.) Flatten the dough into a disk, then wrap in plastic wrap and refrigerate for 30 minutes. Roll the dough into a 12-inch round on a lightly floured surface and fit into a 9-inch pie plate. Crimp the edges and prick the bottom and sides all over with a fork. Line with foil and fill with pie weights. Bake in the middle of your oven for 15 minutes, then carefully remove the foil and weights and bake the shell until pale golden, 5 to 10 minutes more. Cool on a wire rack for 5 minutes.

Filling

- 6 large eggs
- $1^1/2$ cups sugar
- $1/8$ teaspoon salt
- 6 tablespoons well-shaken buttermilk
- 3 tablespoons yellow cornmeal
- 4 teaspoons grated lemon zest
- 6 tablespoons fresh lemon juice
- 1 pinch freshly grated nutmeg
- $1/2$ cup (1 stick) unsalted butter, melted

Preheat the oven to 325°F. Thoroughly whisk together the eggs, sugar, and salt. Whisk in all the remaining ingredients except the butter, then gradually add the butter and whisk until smooth. Pour the filling into the pie shell and cover the edge of the crust with foil to prevent overbrowning. Bake until just set, about 40 minutes, then allow to cool. *Makes one 9-inch single-crust pie.*

SOUTHERN U.S.
KILLER PIES

POOGAN'S PORCH

CHARLESTON, SOUTH CAROLINA

The historic port city of Charleston is famous for its breathtaking Southern architecture dripping with Spanish moss, its quaint sidewalk cafes, and the smell of magnolias in the air. It's also famous for haunted haunts, and as legend has it, one of Charleston's spooky spots also happens to be one of its best restaurants. The ghost in question is Zoe St. Amand, a spinster schoolteacher who reportedly frequents her former residence, 72 Queen Street, now Poogan's Porch. Restaurant employees claim to have witnessed many strange and unexplained things, including heavy kitchen doors slamming shut on their own, framed pictures knocked off walls, and items switching locations in the kitchen. Some people—including restaurant patrons—even claim

to have seen Zoe's spirit. According to local lore, she haunts her former home looking for love and attention, which she apparently died without.

Ghost stories aside, Poogan's Porch is also renowned for its food, which is a mix of Lowcountry cuisine and Southern home cooking, with a multitude of fresh seafood thrown into the mix. The restaurant frequently tops "Best of" lists, and is a favorite with celebrities and politicians. Pastry chef Nicole Anhalt also delights guests with inventive, glorious desserts. One of her favorites, the Kahlúa pecan pie, reflects her Southern upbringing. Pecan pie is a Southern classic, and it's a versatile treat that can be dressed up or down in myriad ways. In this recipe, Anhalt adds a kick of coffee flavor to complement the rich nuts.

Kahlúa Pecan Pie

Filling

3 large eggs

¼ cup (½ stick) unsalted butter, melted

1½ cups light corn syrup

1 tablespoon sugar

¼ cup Kahlúa liqueur

Vanilla extract, to taste

1⅓ cups (5½ ounces) pecan pieces

1 unbaked 9-inch pie shell (page 8)

Preheat the oven to 425°F. Put the eggs in a large bowl and beat slightly. Add the butter, corn syrup, sugar, Kahlúa, and vanilla. Mix well with a whisk. Place the pecans in the bottom of the pie shell to form a layer. (They will float to the top during baking.) Pour the filling on top of the pecans.

Bake the pie for 15 minutes. Reduce the oven temperature to 350°F and bake for an additional 20 to 30 minutes, or until the filling is set but still slightly loose in the center. *Makes one 9-inch single-crust pie.*

GENERAL BAKIN' TIP

★ Everyone longs for a perfect crust, and Nicole Anhalt's secret is simple: Just before you begin to make the filling, place the pie shell in the freezer. When you're finished, pull the shell out of the freezer and add the pecans and filling. The almost-frozen shell will result in a flakier crust.

SOUTHERN U.S. KILLER PIES

CRYSTAL GRILL

GREENWOOD, MISSISSIPPI

Diners entering the Crystal Grill for the first time undoubtedly notice two things: the mosaic tile floor and the pies in the glass display case. Of particular note are the meringue pies, with their skyscraping layers of light-as-air topping slathered generously on beds of creamy filling. These pies just might be the tallest pies in the Deep South.

Before it was the Crystal Grill, the restaurant was the Elite Café, a one-room diner that opened in 1923. Current owner Mike Ballas' brother-in-law purchased it in 1952, changed the name to the Crystal Grill, and eventually sold it to Ballas, who's been running it ever since. His son John now aids his father at the helm, cooking up tamales, shrimp Creole, and other mouthwatering Delta delicacies.

While some things have changed since 1952, such as the addition of more dining rooms and two bars, other things have not—like their pies. The elder Ballas developed the recipe for the coconut meringue pie, and the Crystal Grill has been serving it since 1952. But it's only recently that the pies have been getting a great deal of attention from anyone other than Grill regulars. In just a few short years, they've gone from virtual obscurity to celebrity, courtesy of Jane and Michael Stern's *Roadfood* and National Public Radio. General manager Robert Gillespie doesn't quite get why it's taken more than fifty years for people to notice. "This pie business has all of the sudden just blown up," he says. "I have no idea where it came from. I guess they are interesting to look at."

Coconut Meringue Pie

Crust

> 6 cups pastry flour
>
> 4 cups shortening
>
> Salt, to taste
>
> 2 cups water

Preheat the oven to 350°F. Mix together all the ingredients until the dough forms a ball. Divide into 3 equal parts; freeze 2 parts for later use. Roll 1 part to an 11-inch round, and fit into a 9-inch pie plate. Bake for about 10 minutes, or until golden.

Filling

> 1 cup (2 sticks) unsalted butter
>
> $1\frac{1}{2}$ cups shredded coconut
>
> 3 teaspoons vanilla extract
>
> $\frac{1}{2}$ cup sugar
>
> $1\frac{3}{4}$ cups milk
>
> 5 egg yolks
>
> $\frac{1}{3}$ cup cornstarch

Combine the butter, coconut, vanilla, sugar, and $1\frac{1}{2}$ cups of the milk in a saucepan, and stir over low heat. In a bowl, mix together the egg yolks and cornstarch. Bring the remaining $\frac{1}{4}$ cup milk to a simmer in a separate saucepan. Whisk the hot milk into the egg mixture. Add the milk-egg mixture to the coconut mixture and bring to a boil. Cook for about 2 minutes. Remove from the heat and pour into a bowl. Cover the bowl with a sheet of waxed paper and let cool. Pour the filling into the pie shell.

Meringue

> 5 egg whites
>
> $1\frac{1}{4}$ cups sugar
>
> $\frac{1}{2}$ cup shredded coconut

Beat the egg whites and $\frac{5}{8}$ cup of the sugar with a hand mixer until soft peaks form. Dissolve remaining sugar in enough water to cover the sugar and boil to 240°F. Carefully pour in a slow stream into the egg whites, beating until firm peaks form. Spread the meringue on top of the filling, then sprinkle with the coconut. Bake for 5 to 7 minutes, or until slightly brown. Allow to cool. *Makes one 9-inch single-crust pie, plus dough for 2 more single-crust pies.*

BLUE BONNET CAFÉ

MARBLE FALLS, TEXAS

Since 1929, the Blue Bonnet Café has been serving food to hungry Texans in the town of Marble Falls, situated on the Highland Lakes in central Texas. On weekends, however, Marble Falls' population of five thousand swells to more than 100,000, as vacationers and retirees travel to their lake houses to find respite from the heat. John Kemper, who has owned the café with his wife, Belinda, for twenty-five years, says, "It's a very busy little town, and the Blue Bonnet is a very busy restaurant."

Blue Bonnet customers enter the eatery through a side door, which leads them through a little hallway past the kitchen and into the dining room, and they exit through the front door. When there is a wait for a table—a frequent occurrence—hungry patrons whet their appetites by watching the cooks prepare food through a window in the kitchen door. These ravenous folks feast on specials of chicken-fried steak, Mama's pot roast, grilled liver and onions, and fried okra. And for dessert? Pie is the hands-down favorite. "We're well known for our pie," Kemper says. "Almost everybody eats pie." The Blue Bonnet certainly makes enough to go around; on an average day, they bake fifty to one hundred pies. One of the favorites is coconut cream pie, which Kemper describes as an "icebox pie that people just love."

Coconut Cream Pie

Filling

    1 cup sugar
    ¼ cup cornstarch
    ¼ teaspoon salt
    3 cups milk
    4 egg yolks
    3 tablespoons unsalted butter
    ½ teaspoon vanilla extract
    7 tablespoons flaked coconut

1 fully baked 9-inch pie shell (page 8)

Combine the sugar, cornstarch, salt, and milk. Cook over low to medium heat, stirring constantly. After the mixture bubbles up and thickens, cook an additional 2 minutes, then remove from the heat. Beat the egg yolks slightly, then gradually stir 1 cup of the hot sugar mixture into the yolks. Return the yolk-sugar mixture to the saucepan and bring to a gentle boil. Cook and stir for about 2 minutes, then remove from the heat. Add the butter and vanilla, stirring until the butter melts. Add the coconut. Pour the filling into the pie crust. Let the pie cool in the refrigerator before adding the topping.

Topping

    ½ cup heavy cream
    ½ cup confectioners' sugar
    ½ teaspoon vanilla extract

Beat the cream on high with an electric mixer. As the cream starts to thicken, add the sugar gradually, followed by the vanilla. Beat until soft peaks form, taking care not to overbeat. Add to the top of the pie. *Makes one 9-inch single-crust pie.*

SOUTHERN U.S.
KILLER PIES

ED & KAY'S

BENTON, ARKANSAS

Ed & Kay's has been a Benton staple since 1950, the sort of place where people always run into someone they know who's also dining on chicken-fried steak, pork tenderloin, biscuits and gravy, or cinnamon rolls the size of dinner plates. The central Arkansas town is just twenty-five miles from Little Rock, and Ed & Kay's manager, Phyllis Scott, has noticed a lot more development and growth in the past few years. "The sign says the population is 25,000," she says, "but I'd bet it's about 32,000."

Even with more people, more traffic, and more technology in Benton, Ed & Kay's has taken an old-time approach and preserved what matters most to its customers: good, down-home food and friendly service. "We cut our own meat and make our gravy in a skillet the old-fashioned way," Scott says. What Ed & Kay's is best known for, however, is its pies. Each pie is made from scratch, and they are so popular that an old-fashioned approach to getting them to insatiable customers just wouldn't do. Now Ed & Kay's ships pies—frozen, of course—to all parts of the country, and even overseas.

Some of the restaurant's best-loved pie recipes actually came from customers who shared them with co-owner Kay Diemer. The fudge pie appeared on the menu in exactly this way, though Diemer and company tweaked it a bit to make it an Ed & Kay original. Says manager Scott, "We cut a little here and added a little here. Kay is wonderful in the kitchen. She loves inventing."

Fudge Pie

Filling

2 cups sugar

1 cup (2 sticks) margarine, melted

4 eggs

6 tablespoons all-purpose flour

6 tablespoons unsweetened cocoa powder

1 cup chopped pecans

1 teaspoon vanilla extract

Pinch of salt

1 unbaked 10-inch pie shell (page 8)

Preheat the oven to 325°F. Mix all the filling ingredients together in a large bowl. Pour into the pie crust. Bake for 30 minutes. Allow to cool before serving. *Makes one 10-inch single-crust pie.*

GENERAL BAKIN' TIP

★ This chocolatey dessert is best served with ice cream, fresh whipped cream, or fresh strawberries.

LOUIE'S BACKYARD

KEY WEST, FLORIDA

At the turn of the century, Key West was infamous for being a rough-and-tumble, rowdy town full of sailors, fishermen, and sea captains. One such sea captain was Captain James Randall Adams, who purchased a house on Waddell Street in the early 1900s. Years later, after the town became known for its lush tropical beauty and mostly genteel citizenry, Frances and Louie Signorelli purchased the home from the Adams family and Louie's Backyard opened, boasting the same Doric columns and Bahamian shutters from the days of Captain Adams. According to restaurant lore, the original Louie's had twelve tables, one waiter, and a cigar box that functioned as a cash register.

A fixture on the National Registry of Historic Places since 1984—soon after the Tenneys, the current owners, bought and renovated it—Louie's Backyard is now an altogether different affair. A large deck offers diners a heart-stopping view of the Atlantic Ocean, and the cuisine is high-end. Pastry chef Niall Bowen credits chef Doug Shook with pushing the food at Louie's to greater limits, a sentiment echoed by accolades from the Food Network and *Wine Spectator*, among others.

But Bowen takes all the credit—jokingly but deservedly proud—for Louie's famous Key lime pie, which the restaurant wasn't making at all until Bowen joined the crew in 1998. Of the ten regular desserts on the menu, the Key lime pie brings in 45 percent of the dessert sales, and Bowen bakes ten to fifteen Key lime pies each night. What's most notable about the pie is that it forgoes the traditional graham-cracker crust for a gingersnap crust, which adds an extra bit of spice and balances perfectly with the lime.

Key Lime Pie

Crust

- $2/3$ cup sugar
- 1 cup (2 sticks) unsalted butter, at room temperature
- Pinch of salt
- $3\frac{1}{4}$ cups all-purpose flour
- 2 extra-large eggs
- 1 teaspoon vanilla extract
- $\frac{1}{4}$ cup molasses
- 1 tablespoon ground ginger
- $\frac{1}{2}$ teaspoon ground cinnamon

Preheat the oven to 325°F. Cream the sugar, butter, and salt together in a large bowl until smooth. Add the remaining ingredients and mix until smooth. Roll out the dough on a lightly floured surface, making a round 13 inches across and $\frac{1}{4}$ inch thick. Line a 9-inch tart pan with a removable bottom with the dough. Trim off the excess. Bake for 12 to 15 minutes, or until the crust is nicely brown.

Filling

- One 14-ounce can sweetened condensed milk
- $\frac{1}{2}$ cup fresh Key lime juice or regular lime juice
- 4 extra-large egg yolks
- 1 teaspoon vanilla extract

Combine all the ingredients together with a wire whisk. Pour into the baked pie crust and bake at 325°F until the filling sets into a soft custard, about 15 minutes. Cool completely before cutting.

Raspberry Coulis

- 2 cups fresh or frozen raspberries
- 1 cup sugar
- $\frac{1}{4}$ cup water
- $\frac{1}{8}$ teaspoon vanilla extract

Purée all the ingredients, then strain through a fine sieve. Drizzle in a zigzag across a plate, then place a slice of pie on top. Add a dollop of fresh whipped cream and fresh raspberries to garnish, if desired. *Makes one 9-inch single-crust pie.*

BAYONA

NEW ORLEANS, LOUISIANA

Few foods evoke nostalgia and the feeling of childlike wonder quite like s'mores, a combination of chocolate, graham crackers, and marshmallows that can only be described as divine. Nearly a year after the disaster of Hurricane Katrina swallowed up New Orleans, the French Quarter restaurant Bayona finds itself doing surprisingly well, given its devastated surroundings. Pastry chef Megan Roen Forman, who developed the delectable s'more pie recipe, recalls watching the restaurant slowly grow busier and busier as the days, weeks, and months after the hurricane passed. "I think people really needed to go out," she says. "I think they needed to meet friends, [have a] drink, and have a good time."

A native of New Orleans, Roen Forman spent years honing her craft in New York City, working with the celebrated likes of Richard Leach, François Payard, Jean-Philippe Maury, and Rick Bayless. Her creations have been featured in *Modern Bride* magazine, the *New York Daily News*, and the *New Orleans Culinary Concierge*, and in 2003, Starchefs.com named her a Rising Star Pastry Chef. Pomp and circumstance aside, Roen Forman delighted in creating her version of the gooey campfire treat—a sophisticated dessert that still manages to capture all the feelings of whimsical abandon by mixing the flavors that our inner child holds so near and dear.

S'more Pie

Filling

> 12 ounces bittersweet chocolate, chopped into $\frac{1}{4}$-inch pieces
>
> 2 cups heavy cream

1 prebaked 9-inch graham-cracker pie shell; see tip

Put the chocolate in a mixing bowl. In a saucepan, bring the cream to a boil. Pour over the chocolate and slowly whisk until blended. Pour into the pie shell and refrigerate until set.

Marshmallow Topping

> 3 egg whites
>
> 2 envelopes unflavored gelatin
>
> $\frac{1}{2}$ cup cold water
>
> 2 tablespoons corn syrup
>
> 1 $\frac{1}{2}$ cups sugar

Put the egg whites in the bowl of an electric mixer fitted with a whip attachment. Pour the gelatin into a small bowl, add $\frac{1}{4}$ cup of the water, and stir. In a small saucepan, cook the corn syrup, sugar, and the remaining $\frac{1}{4}$ cup of water until the mixture reaches 240°F. Remove from the stove and stir in the dissolved gelatin. With the mixer on medium-high speed, slowly and carefully pour the cooked sugar down the side of the bowl into the egg whites. When the mixture has cooled slightly—it will hold its shape but won't be set—remove the bowl from the mixer. With a rubber spatula, pile the topping onto the chocolate filling. Refrigerate for 1 hour, or until set. Just before serving, brown the topping under a broiler or with a propane torch. *Makes one 9-inch single-crust pie.*

GENERAL BAKIN' TIP

★ Pre-baked graham-cracker pie shells can be found in the baking-goods section of your local grocery store.

LYNDEN DUTCH BAKERY

LYNDEN, WASHINGTON

Lynden, Washington, has an enchanting storybook quality to it. The town got its name from a verse in the 1803 poem "On the Battle of Hohenlinden," by Thomas Campbell: "On Linden, when the sun was low, / All bloodless lay the untrodden snow, / And dark as winter was the flow / Of Iser rolling rapidly." (The original spelling was changed from an I to a Y because, according to town lore, the Y looked prettier.) Separated from Vancouver Island in Canada by a series of straits, Lynden is a small agricultural community whose mainstays are milk, strawberries, blueberries, and raspberries.

In the early 1900s, the town experienced an influx of immigrants from the Netherlands, and since then has retained and celebrated its predominantly Dutch roots. Downtown Lynden, in fact, could be renamed Little Holland. Many of the townspeople speak Dutch as they dine at one of the Dutch restaurants or pass by the seventy-two-foot windmill. Along with their staff, Lynden Dutch Bakery owners Steve and Rise Copeman whip up homemade cookies, wedding cakes, pastries, breads, and pies with that special Dutch touch. Sour cream raisin pie is a favorite in the Midwest and Pacific Northwest, and the bakery's version is blissful.

Sour Cream Raisin Pie

Filling

 1 1/2 cups raisins

 3 cups sour cream

 9 ounces instant vanilla pudding mix

 1/2 cup granulated sugar

 1/2 teaspoon ground cinnamon

 1/2 teaspoon ground cloves

 1/2 teaspoon ground nutmeg

 1/2 cup (4 ounces) cream cheese, at room temperature

 1/2 cup confectioners' sugar

1 fully baked 9-inch pie shell (page 8)

Soak the raisins in enough lukewarm water to cover for anywhere from 10 minutes to 24 hours. Drain, reserving a bit of liquid to moisten the filling, if necessary. In a large bowl, mix together the sour cream, pudding mix, sugar, and spices. Scrape the bowl and mix thoroughly. Add the raisins and mix lightly. (If the pudding mixture is too thick, add a little reserved raisin-water and mix lightly.) In another bowl, mix the cream cheese and sugar. Spread evenly in the bottom of the pie shell. Spread the pudding mixture on top.

Topping

 1 pint heavy cream or canned whipped cream

 2 tablespoons raisins

Whip the cream, or use canned whipped cream, and completely cover the filling. Sprinkle with the raisins and serve immediately. *Makes one 9-inch single-crust pie.*

GENERAL BAKIN' TIPS

★ For extra flavor, soak the raisins in orange juice, lemonade, or other fruit juice instead of water.

★ Don't skimp on the whipped cream topping. It's a signature of this type of pie and what elevates (literally) this dessert to greatness.

ROSE RIVER INN BED & BREAKFAST

ASTORIA, OREGON

When Pam Armstrong bakes her chocolate pie, she thinks of her grandmother; after all, she's using her recipe. Armstrong, who owns the Rose River Inn Bed & Breakfast in Astoria, Oregon, estimates the recipe is more than fifty years old. "My grandmother made it when she was young, and I made it with her when I was a girl," Armstrong, a former professional cake decorator, says.

Armstrong and her husband, David, relocated from Lodi, California, to Astoria to take over the Rose River Inn Bed & Breakfast, and she brought her grandma's pie recipe with her. Just four blocks from the Columbia River, the inn is a relic of Astoria's past; the

Craftsman-style house was built in 1912. In fact, the whole town is a great spot for history buffs. Part of the Lewis and Clark Trail, Astoria—originally a fur-trading outpost named Fort Astoria—was the first settlement west of the Rockies. At the Rose River Inn, visitors can stay in one of four guest rooms, all of which are cozy, sunny, and filled with primitive country antiques, a décor Armstrong describes as "homey, not a lot of frill-frill."

The recipe for Grandma's chocolate pie doesn't have a lot of "frill-frill," either. The dessert features minimal ingredients and is simple to make. Even more important: It's a chocoholic's dream come true.

Grandma's Chocolate Pie

Filling

    1 cup sugar

    $2\frac{1}{2}$ tablespoons Hershey's cocoa powder

    $2\frac{1}{2}$ tablespoons all-purpose flour or Wondra (instant flour)

    $1\frac{1}{2}$ cups milk

    $\frac{1}{2}$ cup evaporated milk

    3 egg yolks

    1 teaspoon vanilla extract

1 fully baked 9-inch pie shell (page 8)

Mix the sugar, cocoa, and flour together well in a large bowl, then add the milks and egg yolks. In a saucepan, cook the mixture over medium heat, stirring constantly, until thick, then stir in the vanilla extract. Pour the filling into the pie shell and let sit until set, about 3 hours. Top with whipped cream if desired. *Makes one 9-inch single-crust pie.*

GENERAL BAKIN' TIP

★ Pam Armstrong recommends using Pillsbury's premade pie shells.

WESTERN KILLER PIES

NORTH FORK STORE & CAFÉ

NORTH FORK, IDAHO

The North Fork Store & Café is a nifty solution for North Folk, a town found in the heart of an area ominously monikered "River of No Return Wilderness." The long, low building is a combination store, restaurant, post office, laundromat, deli, liquor store, and gas station—one-stop shopping for locals and visitors alike.

In 1805, Meriwether Lewis and William Clark passed through North Fork, Idaho, on their adventurous journey to the Pacific Coast, and the area is now an official designation on the famous Lewis and Clark

Trail. Nowadays, most visitors travel to North Fork to fish in the nearby Salmon River, white-water raft, camp, hike, and generally get away from it all—270 and 230 miles, in fact, from Idaho's largest metropolises, Boise and Pocatello, respectively. Built against the scenic backdrop of the Sawtooth Mountains, the café part of the North Fork Store & Café has been surprising and delighting patrons for years with its food. Plus, the North Fork's raspberry cherry pie is simple, unfussy, but divine—just like a trip to the mountains.

Raspberry Cherry Pie

Filling

 1 1/4 cups frozen sweetened raspberries, thawed but not drained

 2 1/2 cups (15 ounces) canned pitted tart red cherries

 3/4 cup sugar

 3 tablespoons cornstarch

 1/4 teaspoon salt

Double-crust pie dough (page 8)

Milk, for brushing

2 tablespoons sugar, for sprinkling

Preheat the oven to 400°F. Drain the raspberries, reserving the syrup. Drain the cherries, reserving the juice. Add enough cherry juice to the syrup to measure 1 cup liquid. In a saucepan, mix together the sugar, cornstarch, and salt. Stir in the raspberry-cherry liquid, then the cherries. Cook and stir the mixture over medium heat until sugar is dissolved. Remove from heat and stir in the drained raspberries. Return to medium heat and cook 20 minutes longer, stirring occasionally.

On a lightly floured board, roll each disk of dough into an 11-inch round. Fit 1 round into a 9-inch pie pan. Pour the filling into the pie shell and cover with the top crust. Cut vents into the top crust. Brush with the milk and sprinkle with the sugar. Bake for about 1 hour, or until golden brown. *Makes one 9-inch double-crust pie.*

GENERAL BAKIN' TIP

★ If using fresh raspberries, use 1 1/2 cups raspberries and 3/4 cup cherry juice instead of 1 1/4 cups frozen raspberries and 1 cup cherry juice.

INN AT SCHOOLHOUSE CREEK

MENDOCINO, CALIFORNIA

Northern California is a favorite American vacation spot, and travelers adore one of the area's oldest inns for its breathtaking coastal views, compelling history, and owners Maureen Gilbert and Steven Musser's delectable edibles. A few buildings on the property of the Inn at Schoolhouse Creek were built in the 1860s and 1870s. The inn in its current form opened in 1932, coinciding with the completion of the "Shoreline Highway," now known as Highway One. Visitors stay in one of several old cottages with botanical names such as Rose, Heather, Fuchsia, Cypress, Thyme, and Tansy. Other units were built in the 1950s to cater to the motel craze of the era. In the 1970s,

the owner allegedly flew in guests from Las Vegas and Reno to hold high-stakes card games at the inn.

Visitors to the inn can enjoy a ton of different activities, from in-house massages and daily wine hours—featuring local wines from the renowned Anderson Valley wineries—to visits with the owners' menagerie of dogs, chickens, and miniature donkeys, and picnics with made-to-order baskets prepared by Gilbert and Musser. One extra-special treat is the Mississippi comfort pie, which combines the varied flavors and textures of walnuts, coconut, raisins, and rum. The recipe comes from Musser's mother, and was a favorite of his as a child.

Mississippi Comfort Pie

Filling

    1 cup sugar

    $1/2$ cup (1 stick) unsalted butter, at room temperature

    2 eggs, beaten

    1 teaspoon distilled white vinegar

    1 tablespoon dark rum

    $1/2$ cup walnuts

    $1/2$ cup flaked coconut

    $1/2$ cup raisins

1 unbaked 9-inch pie shell (page 8), chilled

Preheat the oven to 325°F. Mix together the sugar, butter, and eggs and beat until smooth. Blend in the vinegar and rum. Stir in the nuts, coconut, and raisins. Pour into the chilled pie shell and bake for 50 minutes. Allow the pie to cool before slicing, and serve. *Makes one 9-inch single-crust pie.*

SWEETIE PIES

NAPA, CALIFORNIA

When the going gets tough, the tough get going. Or, in Toni Chiappetta's case, the tough get baking. In the mid-1990s, Chiappetta found herself out of work, so she found solace in baking cakes in her very tiny apartment kitchen. The solace was short-lived, however, as her oven was only big enough to hold one cake at a time; the idea for the next step on her career path came in a flash. She began baking regularly, sending out samples to local companies, and within four months was able to move her operation to a commercial kitchen with ovens large enough to bake several cakes, pies, muffins, and other sweet treats at once. In 2000, Chiappetta and her loyal and trusty crew opened Sweetie Pies in Napa.

Wine tends to get all the attention in that neck of the Northern California woods, but the desserts here are nothing short of divine. At Sweetie Pies, people don't use words such as "legs" or "bouquet" or "nose" to describe the fare. Just one word will suffice—"delicious." Folks in Napa flock to Sweetie Pies for breakfast muffins, savory tarts and quiches, soups, and panini in addition to their scrumptious desserts and pastry. The glass display cases in the cozy shop are filled with decadent delights—two-layer chocolate opera cakes filled with creamy mousse, bread pudding, whoopee pies, turnovers, fresh-baked cookies, and more. And let's not forget the pies, particularly the chocolate pecan pie, which features the flavors of not only chocolate and pecans but also maple syrup.

Chocolate Pecan Pie

Crust

>   2 cups all-purpose flour
> $\frac{1}{2}$ teaspoon salt
>   1 cup (2 sticks) plus $\frac{1}{2}$ tablespoon unsalted butter, cut into cubes and frozen
>   2 egg yolks
>   4 to 6 tablespoons cold water

Preheat the oven to 350°F. Put the flour and salt in the bowl of a stand mixer or food processor and mix on low speed to combine. Add the butter and continue to mix on low until the mixture resembles coarse meal. Add the egg yolks and enough water for the dough to just come together. Remove from the bowl, form into a disk, wrap in plastic wrap, and refrigerate for at least 30 minutes. Remove the dough from the refrigerator, put on a floured surface, and roll into a circle about $\frac{1}{4}$ inch thick and 13 inches in diameter. Fit into a 10-inch pie pan. Cut the overhang to 1 inch from the lip of the pan. Turn the excess dough under until it sits on the edge of the pan. Place the pie shell in the freezer for at least 1 hour. Remove from the freezer and line with aluminum foil, making sure to press the foil securely into the bottom crease and to cover the edges of the crust. Fill with pie weights and bake for 15 to 20 minutes, or until the bottom is dry and slightly golden brown. Remove the foil and weights and bake for 3 to 5 minutes. Let cool.

Filling

>   6 eggs
>   1 cup sugar
> $\frac{1}{4}$ cup light corn syrup
> $\frac{3}{4}$ cup maple syrup
> $\frac{1}{4}$ cup unsalted butter, melted
> $\frac{1}{3}$ cup bittersweet chocolate chips
> $2\frac{1}{2}$ cups pecan halves

In a bowl, whisk together the eggs, sugar, and syrups. Add butter and whisk, then stir in the chocolate chips. Spread the pecans in the bottom of the pie crust. Pour the filling on top, making sure that the chocolate chips are evenly distributed. Bake for 50 to 60 minutes, or until the sides are set and slightly puffed up. Remove from the oven and cool before serving. Garnish with chopped nuts, melted chocolate, and whipped cream if desired. *Makes one 10-inch single-crust pie.*

WALNUT CAFÉ

BOULDER, COLORADO

Dana Derichsweiler—or, as most people in Boulder know her, Dana D.—may be a Rocky Mountain dweller, but she hasn't lost a bit of her Texas charm and hospitality. It's what keeps people coming back to her restaurant, the Walnut Café, which she has operated for more than twenty years.

Dana brought to Boulder her Southern family's love of, and some of their recipes for, pie. Every Tuesday at the Walnut Café is Pie Day, where slices of homemade pie are a dollar off. Dana takes pie requests, and bakes recipes that come from her customers' families. Some lucky folks even get pies named after them. All of this,

she says, has contributed to an already existent "underground pie culture" in Boulder. "Some people will come in here and order two or three slices of pie; that's breakfast or that's lunch," she says.

Her chess pie recipe originated from her family in Texas, but over the years she's "messed with it" a bit, in turn educating Boulder residents who had never heard of the Southern classic. "My mom made chess pie for her bridge club in the '60s," she reminisces. "It filled the house with the smell of vanilla. I call it a 'sippin' pie.' It's so dense and rich that you take one bite, sip your black coffee, then take another bite."

Old-Fashioned Chess Pie

Filling

    $\frac{1}{2}$ cup heavy cream

    1 tablespoon fresh lemon juice

    $\frac{1}{2}$ teaspoon vanilla extract

    3 egg yolks

    1 egg

    1 cup sugar

    $\frac{1}{4}$ cup cornmeal

    $\frac{1}{4}$ teaspoon salt

    $\frac{1}{2}$ cup (1 stick) unsalted butter, melted

1 unbaked 9-inch pie shell (page 8)

Whipped cream

Preheat the oven to 350°F. Beat together the cream, lemon juice, and vanilla extract. Add the egg yolks, egg, sugar, cornmeal, salt, and butter. Beat until the mixture is thick but not foamy.

Pour the filling into the pie crust and bake for 45 to 50 minutes, or until the filling is set and golden brown. Serve warm or cold, with whipped cream. *Makes one 9-inch single-crust pie.*

THE FAMOUS PLAZA RESTAURANT

— SANTA FE, NEW MEXICO —

It's known as both the Plaza Restaurant and the Famous Plaza Café, but one thing is for certain: People in Santa Fe love the food served at 54 Lincoln Avenue. Situated smack-dab in the town square (known as the Plaza), the Famous Plaza Restaurant has been open since 1918. The current owners, the Razatos family, took it over in 1947, and the eatery has managed to retain its retro charm, while the scores of photographs of New Mexico remind patrons of its long, illustrious history.

Sure, America is the world's favorite melting pot, but the Famous Plaza Restaurant's menu might be a close second. Certainly much of the food is inspired by New Mexico's neighbors south of the border, but diners can just as easily order a Greek salad or an omelet as they can an enchilada. Many favorite dishes seem to be informed by an array of cultures—diner culture included. Hash browns, flapjacks, and what is widely considered the best cup of coffee in Santa Fe all converge at the Plaza.

The Plaza's apple pie is another fine example of cross-cultural gastronomy. At first glance, it looks like your standard American classic. But Plaza owner Andy Razatos and his family serve the pie with *cajeta*, a fresh, homemade variation of *dulce de leche*, a Latin counterpart to whipped cream. *Cajeta*, or caramelized sweetened milk, can be found in a Latino grocery or section of your local supermarket, but the Plaza recipe remains a well-guarded secret.

Apple Pie

Crust

   $4\frac{1}{2}$ cups all-purpose flour

   2 tablespoons sugar

   2 teaspoons salt

   $\frac{1}{2}$ cup (1 stick) unsalted butter, cut into 1-inch squares and frozen for 2 hours

   $\frac{1}{2}$ cup vegetable shortening, cut into 1-inch squares and frozen for 2 hours

   1 cup ice water

Combine the flour, sugar, and salt in a bowl or food processor. Add the butter and shortening and mix until it resembles coarse cornmeal. Add the water and mix just until the dough comes together. (The butter and shortening should still be visible.) Cut the dough into equal halves, flatten, wrap in plastic wrap, and refrigerate for 30 minutes.

Filling

   12 Granny Smith apples, peeled, cored, and sliced

   2 cups packed brown sugar

   1 tablespoon ground cinnamon

   1 cup pecans

   1 cup all-purpose flour

1 egg
1 teaspoon water
Brown sugar, for sprinkling

Preheat the oven to 350°F. Mix all the filling ingredients together. On a lightly floured surface, roll out 1 half of the dough into a $\frac{1}{8}$-inch-thick 10-inch round. Repeat for the top crust. Fit 1 pastry round into a 9-inch pie pan. Pour in the filling, forming it into a mound, then place the top crust on top. Press the edges of the bottom and top crusts together into a $\frac{1}{2}$-inch lip standing up around the edge of the pan. Bend the lip of the dough into an evenly spaced fluted design. Mix together the egg and water to form an egg wash. Brush the top of the pie with the egg wash and sprinkle generously with brown sugar. Bake for 1 hour and 20 minutes, or until the juices are bubbling. Top with *cajeta*. *Makes one 9-inch double-crust pie.*

THE BORDER GRILL

SANTA MONICA, CALIFORNIA

When Mary Sue Milliken and Susan Feniger met in 1978 while working at the Chicago restaurant Le Perroquet, they formed an instant bond. They were the only two women in an all-male kitchen, and even when they went their separate ways, they knew their paths would cross again. Little did the French-trained chefs know that their careers would soon become intertwined around Mexican food.

In the past twenty-five-plus years, Milliken and Feniger (better known as the "Too Hot Tamales" of Food Network and cookbook fame) have opened five restaurants. While their first two eateries blended flavors from all corners of the globe, the remaining three—Border Grill in Santa Monica, Border Grill in Las Vegas, and Cuidad in Los Angeles—focus squarely on food from south of the border.

One of these delicacies is Mexican chocolate cream pie, which is at once authentic and inventive. The crust, for example, is actually an almond meringue, and instead of using real Mexican chocolate, which is difficult to melt, Milliken and Feniger blend two types of chocolate with cinnamon and vanilla to produce the same flavor. Milliken says, "We're not fussy. We love to eat; that's why we became chefs. We encourage people to try to keep it as simple yet as satisfying as you can, to get in the kitchen and cook and enjoy."

Mexican Chocolate Cream Pie

Meringue Shell

    3 large egg whites

    $1/2$ teaspoon cream of tartar

    $3/4$ cup sugar

Preheat the oven to 350°F. Butter the bottom and sides, but not the lip, of a 9-inch glass pie plate. Put the egg whites in a large bowl and carefully set the bowl over a pan of hot water, stirring until slightly warmed. Beat the warm egg whites with an electric mixer until soft peaks form. Beat in the cream of tartar, then add the sugar in a slow, steady stream. Beat constantly, for 15 to 20 minutes longer, or until the mixture is stiff and glossy. Make a pie shell with the meringue by smoothing it over the bottom and sides of the buttered pie plate. Bake until slightly crisp and dry, about 15 minutes. Cool on a wire rack.

Filling

    7 ounces semisweet chocolate, chopped

    1 ounce unsweetened chocolate, chopped

    $2 1/4$ cups cold heavy cream

    $1/3$ cup confectioners' sugar

    $1/4$ teaspoon ground cinnamon

    $1/4$ teaspoon vanilla extract

    $1/2$ cup slivered almonds, toasted and cooled

4 to 6 ounces bittersweet chocolate, grated or shaved into curls (see page 95)

Combine the semisweet and unsweetened chocolates in a bowl over simmering water, stirring occasionally until melted. Let cool to room temperature. Combine the heavy cream, sugar, cinnamon, and vanilla in a bowl. Beat on medium speed until very soft peaks form, 2 to 3 minutes. Stir one-third of the whipped cream mixture into the melted chocolate. Fold in the remaining whipped cream until completely incorporated. Scatter the toasted almonds over the cooked meringue shell, then top with the chocolate-cream filling, smoothing the top. Cover and refrigerate for at least 1 hour before serving. Decorate with grated chocolate or chocolate curls. *Makes one 9-inch pie.*

THE DAILY PIE CAFÉ

PIE TOWN, NEW MEXICO

On the Continental Divide in the New Mexico desert is a township called Pie Town. Route 60 passes straight through, offering the only entrance and exit, and native piñon trees and gnarled junipers offer a tease of vegetation. The name may sound make-believe, but it isn't. As legend has it, in the early 1920s, a Texan named Clyde Norman settled on a bit of land in New Mexico and opened a general store, where he enjoyed baking pies from scratch. Down-on-their-luck Dust Bowlers traveling west from Texas and Oklahoma began calling the area Pie Town because of Norman, and in 1927, when the locals petitioned for a post office, they decided to call it that officially.

Pie is no less important today than it was back then. The town has an annual Pie Festival, in which residents can bake pies, eat pies, and vote for a pie king and queen. They can also eat pie daily at the Daily Pie Café, where there's never any doubt that pie will be on the menu. In fact, a large, hanging "Pie Chart" features a special coding system to alert customers how much of their favorite pies are still available. And we're not talking about a couple different kinds of pie; we're talking about about a wide variety: strawberry rhubarb, triple berry, chocolate-chunk crème, chocolate walnut, and boysenberry, to name a few. Plus, the café makes a famous New Mexican apple pie, which includes the unexpected but indigenous flavors of green chile and piñon nuts. Any kind of pine nut will do for this recipe, and most can be found in the baking section of supermarkets.

New Mexican Apple Pie

Filling

   4 large Granny Smith apples, peeled, cored, and sliced

   1 cup sugar

   3 tablespoons all-purpose flour

   2 teaspoons ground cinnamon

   $3/4$ teaspoon ground nutmeg

   $1/2$ cup frozen or canned chopped green chiles, hot or mild to taste

   Lemon juice, for sprinkling

Put the apple slices in a large bowl. Top with all the remaining ingredients, except the lemon juice, and mix well. Sprinkle the lemon juice over the apples to prevent browning. Set aside to allow the mixture to blend while the crust is being prepared.

Crust

   $2 1/2$ cups all-purpose flour

   $1/8$ teaspoon baking powder

   $1/2$ teaspoon salt

   $1/4$ cup ($1/2$ stick) cold salted butter

   $1/4$ cup vegetable shortening

   1 egg

   1 teaspoon distilled white vinegar

   $1/2$ cup cold water

   $3/4$ cup piñon nuts

Combine the flour, baking powder, and salt in a large bowl. Cut in the butter and shortening. In a separate bowl, mix together the egg, vinegar, and water. Add to the flour mixture and blend with your hands until moist; add more water if needed. Preheat the oven to 425°F. Divide the dough into 2 sections. On a floured board, roll out each section into 11-inch rounds, fit 1 round into a 9-inch pie pan, and spread the piñon nuts evenly in the bottom. Mound the filling on top. Place the second pastry round on top. Flute the edges and cut vent holes in the top crust. Bake for 15 minutes, then reduce the temperature to 400°F and continue baking for 1 hour, or until the juices bubble around the outer edge. *Makes one 9-inch double-crust pie.*

PIE IN THE SKY

— SCOTTSDALE, ARIZONA —

The maxim for Scottsdale's Pie in the Sky—"a slice of heaven"—which accompanies their logo, featuring a cupid delivering a pie, pretty much says it all. Owner Patty Daniels opened Pie in the Sky after her young daughter urged her on, and since then, the bakery has become nothing short of an oasis for Arizona pie fans. Daniels and her crew bake a variety of sweet pies, including standards such as apple and banana cream, as well as more unexpected choices, such as black-bottom praline cream and a ricotta pie studded with nuts, raisins, and a bit of citrus. There are savory pies and quiches, too.

With her baking, Daniels uses both her taste buds and her conscience as guides. The chicken potpie, for example, uses free-range chicken. Everything is made from scratch with cage-free eggs, real butter, and fresh (often organic and local) fruit. The pies are free of any preservatives or other processed or artificial ingredients. Of her peach pie, Daniels says, "The month of May is peach season in Arizona. This recipe allows the simple, fresh flavor of the sweet peaches to come through." Though this pie is best when served the day it is made, it can be refrigerated until it's gone—which probably won't be long.

Peach Pie

Crust

> 3⅓ cups all-purpose flour
>
> ¼ cup sugar
>
> 1¾ cups (3½ sticks) cold unsalted butter, cut into small pieces
>
> ¼ cup ice water

Combine the flour and sugar in a bowl. Add the butter and use your fingers to mix it in until combined, then stir in the ice water. Form the dough into a single ball, wrap in plastic wrap, and refrigerate for at least 30 minutes. Roll half the dough on a lightly floured surface into a round ⅛ inch thick. Fit into a 9-inch pie pan. Roll out the second half for the top crust and set aside.

Filling

> 3 pounds fresh peaches
>
> ¾ cup sugar
>
> ¼ cup cornstarch or all-purpose flour
>
> ¼ teaspoon vanilla extract
>
> Squeeze of fresh lemon juice
>
> 2 tablespoons unsalted butter

1 egg, beaten
Sugar, for sprinkling

Preheat the oven to 350°F. Peel the peaches by scoring an X on the bottom of each, immersing them in boiling water for 20 seconds, and then immediately immersing them in a large bowl of ice water. Peel the skin; it should come off easily. Cut the peaches in half to remove the pit, then cut into thick slices. Toss the slices with the sugar, cornstarch, vanilla, and lemon. Pour the filling into the crust, dotting the top with butter. Brush the overhanging edge of the crust with half of the beaten egg and cover with the top crust. Seal the edges by crimping, and cut several vents in the top. (You can also cut the top crust into strips and place the strips on the pie to form a lattice.) Brush the top crust with the remaining egg and sprinkle with sugar. Bake for 45 to 55 minutes, or until golden brown and the juices are bubbling. Let cool, and serve with fresh whipped cream or vanilla bean ice cream, if desired. *Makes one 9-inch double-crust pie.*

VI'S FOR PIES

EDMONTON, ALBERTA

Almonds, with their salty, subtle nuttiness, are absolutely delicious and much less pedestrian than most nuts, so it's no wonder patrons of Vi's for Pies think their almond chocolate pie is out of this world. This scrumptious pie is the creation of Cheryll Fedorkiw, the owner and pastry chef at Vi's for Pies. After receiving a degree in culinary arts and baking at the Northern Alberta Institute of Technology, Fedorkiw joined the staff of Vi's for Pies, and, seven years later, bought the establishment. While she maintains the original vision for Vi's—to make it a trendy "pie and coffee" café in the upscale Glenora neighborhood of Edmonton—Fedorkiw has expanded the menu in recent years to include sandwiches, pastas, soups, and other homemade dishes.

Just as inviting as the food of Vi's for Pies is the atmosphere. It boasts one of the city's favorite al fresco spots: a cozy, private patio. Inside, the café is warm and comfortable. Diners can sit by the fireplace or in front of the large front window, which looks out at the park-like, tree-lined neighborhood. Fedorkiw and her small staff have not neglected the café's eponymous pies, and people keep coming back for more, frequently commenting that Fedorkiw's pies remind them of the pies their mothers used to make. Her response to compliments often is, "Well, it must be the cup of love I added to the recipe."

Maybe so, but in regards to this pie, named for a friend of Fedorkiw's who has since passed away, the chocolate, almonds, marshmallow, and coconut don't hurt, either.

Sadie's Almond Chocolate Pie

Crust

> **2 cups chocolate cookie crumbs**
> **$\frac{1}{2}$ cup shredded coconut**
> **$\frac{1}{2}$ cup chopped almonds, toasted**
> **$\frac{3}{4}$ cup (1$\frac{1}{2}$ sticks) unsalted butter, melted**

Mix together all the ingredients. Press into the bottom and up the sides of a 9-inch pie plate.

Filling

> **16 ounces semi-sweet chocolate, chopped**
> **16 large marshmallows**
> **$\frac{1}{2}$ cup half-and-half**
> **$\frac{1}{2}$ cup chopped almonds, toasted**
> **1 pint heavy cream**

Toasted sliced almonds, for garnish
Shredded coconut, for garnish

In a saucepan, heat the chocolate, marshmallows, and half-and-half over low heat. Stir until smooth. Stir in the almonds. Refrigerate until cool to the touch, about 1 hour. Whip the cream, then fold into the chocolate mixture. Pour into the crust and refrigerate overnight. Garnish with toasted almonds and coconut. *Makes one 9-inch single-crust pie.*

BLACK CAT GUEST RANCH

HINTON, ALBERTA

Like maple-syrup pie, saskatoon pie is distinctly Canadian. Saskatoon berries, indigenous to the northern and prairie regions of Canada and the northwestern and north-central United States, are prized for their subtle berry-almond flavor. In early spring, white flowers begin to appear on saskatoon shrubs, and the small purple berries ripen in June and July. Amber Hayward, one of the owners of the Black Cat Guest Ranch in Alberta, picks her own berries on the ranch's property for pies she bakes and serves to guests—sometimes at risk of life and limb. "This is a mainstay food for bears in the late summer," she says, "and we often run into them if we go picking berries."

The ranch is located outside the town of Hinton, near Jasper National Park. The ranch got its name from nearby Black Cat Mountain where, in 1885, a fire ravaged the mountain and only a stand of spruce trees was left intact. These surviving trees made a pattern on the mountain that resembled a black cat arching its back. The ranch is one of the oldest of its kind in Alberta, and features sixteen guest rooms and a breathtaking view of the Rocky Mountains. Visitors can participate in a number of outdoor activities, such as horseback riding, hiking, and cross-country skiing. Those who prefer to stay indoors can partake in a writing, photography, or scrapbooking workshop, or participate in one of the ranch's spooky murder-mystery weekends. But whatever activity they choose, visitors often end the day with a slice of this scrumptious pie.

Saskatoon Pie

Filling

    4 cups fresh saskatoon berries

    $\frac{1}{2}$ cup raspberry or orange juice

    1 cup sugar

    3 tablespoons all-purpose flour

    Dash of salt

    Dash of grated nutmeg

    1 tablespoon butter

Double-crust pie dough (page 8)

1 tablespoon unsalted butter

2 tablespoons cream

2 tablespoons sugar

Preheat the oven to 425°F. Mix the berries and juice in a large bowl. In a separate bowl, combine the sugar, flour, salt, and nutmeg and mix into the berries.

On a lightly floured board, roll each disk of dough into an 11-inch round, fitting the first round into a 9-inch pie pan. Pour the filling into pie crust. Dot with the butter. Cut small holes into the second pastry round and place on top of the filling. Seal the edges well, brush the top with cream, and sprinkle with the sugar. Bake for 15 minutes. Reduce the oven temperature to 350°F and bake until nicely browned and the juices begins to bubble through the holes. *Makes one 9-inch double-crust pie.*

GENERAL BAKIN' TIPS

★ If you can't find fresh saskatoon berries, you can purchase ready-made saskatoon pie filling from a number of online purveyors.

★ Use a thimble to cut holes in the top crust to ensure the right size for venting.

JUST DESSERTS CAFÉ

WINNIPEG, MANITOBA

Despite what its name implies, you can eat more than just desserts at Just Desserts Café in Winnipeg, but according to owner Sandy Nicoll, the desserts are the "shining stars."

Situated in Winnipeg's Old Saint-Boniface section, known as the city's French Quarter, this café features a dining room, patio, and gift boutique. Nicoll describes her café as "whimsical and enchanting, yet smartly casual." All menu items, including soups, sandwiches, salads, crepes, pastas, and, naturally, desserts, are made from scratch and are additive- and preservative-free. Nicoll and her staff try to use as many local and organic ingredients as possible. Additionally, Nicoll says, "Just Desserts Café is committed to supporting community events and social causes, and is one of only a handful of restaurants in Winnipeg to have a full-fledged recycling program."

Nicoll learned how to bake by assisting her mother and grandmother in their kitchens, and owning an eatery was a lifelong dream of Nicoll's that finally came true in 1998. Nicoll infused the old-fashioned, from-scratch baking credo she learned from her family's matriarchs into her café's desserts. The result? Sweets that are rich and sinful, as the best ones always are. The hometown darling is the Manitoba maple-walnut pie, which combines the Canadian favorite, maple syrup, with brown sugar, toasted walnuts, and high-quality Belgian milk chocolate.

Manitoba Maple-Walnut Pie

Filling

    3 eggs

    $1/2$ cup maple syrup

    $1/2$ cup maple liqueur

    $1/2$ cup packed brown sugar

    2 teaspoons vanilla extract

    $1/3$ cup unsalted butter, melted

    1 teaspoon maple extract

    $1^1/2$ cups walnuts, toasted and coarsely chopped

    1 cup $1/2$-inch chunks Belgian milk chocolate

1 unbaked 9-inch deep-dish pie shell (page 8); see tip

Preheat the oven to 350°F. In a large bowl, whisk together the eggs, maple syrup, maple liqueur, brown sugar, vanilla extract, butter, and maple extract. When the mixture is well whisked, stir in the nuts and chocolate. Pour into the pie shell and bake for 30 to 45 minutes. The filling may still be a little soft in the middle, but the outside should be fairly firm. Cool on a wire rack. Serve warm, with ice cream. Refrigerate leftovers—if there are any! *Makes one 9-inch single-crust pie.*

GENERAL BAKIN' TIPS

★ Roll the pastry dough out to 14 inches for a deep-dish pie.

★ Maple extract and liqueur can be found at specialty-food shops or purchased online at gourmet websites.

★ Although Sandy Nicoll doesn't garnish her Manitoba maple-walnut pie with chocolate curls, she does use them on many other desserts. To make big curls, microwave a large slab of high-quality chocolate, such as Lindt or Callebaut, on high for 10-second intervals until the chocolate warms slightly. Use a vegetable peeler along the edge of the slab to "peel" off curls.

ABERDEEN MANSION

— VANCOUVER, BRITISH COLUMBIA —

Visitors to Vancouver's Aberdeen Mansion might be tempted to stay a little longer if host Penny Engleman decides to serve her peanut butter pie. The easy-to-make and impossible-to-resist frozen treat is a perfect dessert when temperatures are rising—and, really, any time cravings for peanut butter and chocolate arise.

Aberdeen Mansion is a bed-and-breakfast located just two miles from downtown Vancouver, and a few blocks from the city's bustling and eclectic Commercial Drive district. The B&B is housed in a historic, lovingly restored 1905 home with stained-glass windows, hardwood floors, rooms full of antiques, and guest suites with proper-sounding British names such as Tipperary, Abby, Canterbury, Newcastle, and Belmont, the latter of which features a turn-of-the-century oak fireplace.

A peek outside will delight guests with Vancouver's spectacular scenic beauty.

If you prefer not to do your own cooking in your room's fully equipped kitchen, Engleman's delicious treats and the mansion's close proximity to a bevy of restaurants and cafés providing every type of cuisine imaginable make dining as easy as, well, pie. No matter what you choose to eat for dinner, chances are you'll return to your home-away-from-home for a slice of one of Aberdeen's scrumptious desserts. What makes Aberdeen Mansion's frozen peanut butter pie even more of a treat for the baker is its use of common ingredients that you might already have in your pantry and refrigerator at home. Assembly is a breeze, too: Just put it together and freeze.

Frozen Peanut Butter Pie

Crust

$^1/_3$ cup unsalted butter

One 6-ounce package semisweet chocolate chips

2$^1/_2$ cups Kellogg's Rice Krispies cereal

Melt the butter and chocolate chips in a heavy saucepan over low heat. Remove from the heat and gently stir in the Rice Krispies until they are completely coated. Press into the bottom and up the sides of a buttered 9-inch pie plate. Chill for 30 minutes.

Filling

One 8-ounce package cream cheese, at room temperature

One 10-ounce can sweetened condensed milk

$^3/_4$ cup peanut butter

2 tablespoons fresh lemon juice

1 teaspoon vanilla extract

1 cup heavy cream

Chocolate fudge sauce, for drizzling

Beat the cream cheese in a large bowl until fluffy. Gradually beat in the condensed milk and peanut butter until smooth. Stir in the lemon juice and vanilla. Whip the cream and fold into the peanut butter mixture. Pour into the crust. Drizzle the fudge sauce over the pie and freeze for 4 hours, or until firm. Leftovers may be wrapped and returned to the freezer. *Makes one 9-inch single-crust pie.*

CASCADIA BAKERY

VICTORIA, BRITISH COLUMBIA

The Cascadia Bakery is one of those places that you can't not go into when you walk by. The aroma of freshly baked breads and desserts and the hip-casual vibe beckon passersby, daring them to resist. If the smell doesn't get you through the front door, the sight of relaxed patrons sipping coffee and digging into homemade cakes, breads, and pies at the sidewalk tables will.

And, really, who could resist? Cascadia's breads are hand-shaped, preservative-free, and baked fresh every day. The wide variety of flavors includes rosemary-garlic focaccia, sun-dried tomato, kalamata olive, cinnamon-raisin swirl, and the hearty stone loaf, made with flax seeds, sunflower seeds, organic whole-wheat flour, honey, and just a touch of lemon.

For dessert, from-scratch fruit pies with homey lattice tops, along with old-fashioned carrot cake, chocolate-espresso cheesecake with hazelnut crust, a vegan Belgian-chocolate fudge cake, and brandied chocolate mousse torte, tempt sweet tooths.

According to general manager Zoe O'Doherty, one of the most popular of Cascadia's pies is the raspberry-rhubarb, which melds sweet and tart together. You don't have to make a lattice top, but this presentation is true to Cascadia Bakery and looks all the more rustic and inviting.

Raspberry-Rhubarb Pie

Double-crust pie dough (page 8)

Preheat the oven to 375°F. Lightly spray a 10-inch deep-dish pie plate with cooking spray. Separate one-third of the dough and set aside. Roll the remaining two-thirds of the dough into a $\frac{1}{4}$-inch-thick round on a well-floured surface. Gently fold the round in half and lift onto the pie plate, unfold, and carefully fit into the plate. Trim the excess dough, leaving a 1-inch overhang. Gently roll the overhang under itself to match the edge of the the pie plate. Flute the edge or keep it plain, whichever you prefer. Set aside in refrigerator until ready to fill.

Filling

> $3\frac{1}{2}$ **cups fresh or frozen rhubarb, diced into $\frac{3}{4}$-inch pieces**
> $1\frac{1}{2}$ **cups fresh or frozen raspberries**
> $\frac{3}{4}$ **cup granulated sugar**
> $\frac{1}{4}$ **cup cornstarch**
> **2 teaspoons grated orange zest**

$\frac{1}{4}$ **cup milk**
1 tablespoon raw sugar

In a large bowl, combine the rhubarb, raspberries, granulated sugar, cornstarch, and zest. Stir gently to avoid crushing the raspberries, but make sure the cornstarch is evenly distributed. Pour the filling into the pie crust and level with a spoon or offset spatula to create a flat surface for the lattice top. Roll the remaining one-third of the pastry into a $\frac{1}{4}$-inch-thick round. Cut 1-inch strips with either a paring knife or pastry wheel. Lattice the strips on the pie, leaving space in between the lattice for steam to vent. Trim off any pastry strips at the inside edge of the pie plate. Brush the top with the milk and sprinkle with the raw sugar. Bake for 40 to 50 minutes. The filling should look thick and bubbly at the edges of the pie. Eat it warm, or allow to cool for 2 to 3 hours for a firmly set pie. *Makes one 10-inch latticed pie.*

RESTAURANT AUX ANCIENS CANADIENS

── QUEBEC CITY, QUEBEC ──

Nothing says "O, Canada!" quite like the maple leaf. The maple tree's other by-product, its syrup, is also distinctly Canadian, and it's not only perfect to pour over flapjacks and into oatmeal, it also makes a great pie. One of the best maple-syrup pies in all of Canada can be found at Restaurant Aux Anciens Canadiens in the heart of old Quebec City. Patrons to the eatery are greeted with a cherry *"Bonjour!"* or *"Bonsoir!"* and feast on hearty dinners of game, such as grilled breast of pheasant, caribou in a creamy blueberry-wine sauce, and duck braised in maple-syrup sauce. Manager Serge Duval describes the menu as "French-Canadian food, like our grandmothers made." The restaurant itself is

an impressive as the menu. The building in which it is housed was built in 1675, and the five dining rooms feature five distinct collections of antiquities: wood carvings, china, wooden tools, ancient iron antiques, and a gallery of paintings. The servers even wear authentic seventeenth-century costumes.

Despite the belt buckle–busting fare, most patrons manage to save room for dessert. The most popular is the aforementioned maple-syrup pie (or, *tarte au sirop d'érable*), served with crème fraîche or unsweetened whipped cream. Duval says, "Most pies in Quebec are made with brown sugar and are called sugar pies, but the maple syrup makes it more rich and more authentic."

Maple Syrup Pie

Pie shell dough (page 8)

Preheat the oven to 350°F. Roll the dough into an 11-inch round on a lightly floured surface, and fit it into an 8-inch glass pie plate. Trim to a 1-inch overhang and flute the edges.

Filling
- 1½ cups packed light brown sugar
- 2 large eggs, at room temperature
- ½ cup heavy cream
- ⅓ cup pure maple syrup, preferably Grade A dark amber
- 2 teaspoons unsalted butter, melted

Crème fraîche or unsweetened whipped cream

Whisk together the brown sugar and eggs until creamy. Add the cream, maple syrup, and butter, then whisk until smooth. Pour into the pie shell.

Bake pie at 350°F in the lower third of the oven for 50 to 60 minutes, or until the crust is golden and the filling is puffed and looks dry but still trembles. Cool on a wire rack to room temperature, and the filling will set as the pie cools. Serve with crème fraîche or unsweetened whipped cream. *Makes one 8-inch single-crust pie.*

GENERAL BAKIN' TIPS

★ Be sure to use pure maple syrup; mass-marketed American brands made to top pancakes and waffles are far too sweet and are, well, just not the real thing.

★ If you don't have an 8-inch pie plate, substitute a 9-inch tart pan and partially bake the crust (see page 8) before baking with the filling.

HEARTWOOD BAKERY & CAFÉ

HALIFAX, NOVA SCOTIA

When we think of pies, we tend to think of old-style crusts made with butter or lard, or both. Heartwood Bakery & Café in Halifax, Nova Scotia, proves that you don't need to use animal products to make a darn good pie. Heartwood has been an institution in Halifax for more than a decade, and owner Laura Bishop and her crew are committed to making foods that are meat-free and tasty. The café serves vegetarian and vegan entrees such as moussaka, minty quinoa tabbouleh, and roasted tofu Stroganoff. They bake authentic, 100 percent organic sourdough breads, which they sell from their storefront and at various groceries and wellness centers in the Halifax area. Says Bishop, "All of our foods are prepared on the premises with pure, unrefined ingredients and tender, loving care. Healthy food, healthy people, and a healthy environment are our goals."

After one bite of Heartwood's apple crumble pie, hazelnut torte, pecan pie, or very berry pie, you won't miss those customary ingredients. That said, baking a pie without eggs, milk, butter, or lard requires the use of some unusual ingredients to create good flavor and texture. Heartwood's recipe for very berry pie includes a few: powdered agar, a natural gelatin made from seaweed, and arrowroot, which acts as a thickening agent in the filling. Never fear—your local natural foods store should have everything you need.

Very Berry Pie

Crust

1 3/4 cups organic light spelt flour

Pinch of sea salt

1/3 cup plus 1 tablespoon unrefined corn or safflower oil

1/4 cup plus 2 teaspoons cold water

Put the flour and sea salt in a bowl. Mix the oil and water in a separate bowl. Using a fork, gently mix in the flour to form a soft ball of dough. Roll the dough out on a lightly floured board into a 12-inch round. Fit into a 9-inch pie plate. Trim the overhang to 1 inch and flute the edges.

Tofu Layer

1/2 pound semi-firm plain organic tofu

Grated zest of 1/2 organic orange (optional)

Pinch of sea salt

1/2 teaspoon vanilla extract

1/4 cup plus 1 tablespoon maple syrup

Preheat the oven to 350°F. Mix all the ingredients in a food processor until smooth and creamy. Spread evenly into the pie crust. Bake for 18 to 20 minutes, or until the crust is crisp.

Berry Filling

2 1/4 cups organic unsweetened mixed-berry juice

2 teaspoons powdered agar

1/2 cup maple syrup

1/3 cup arrowroot

1 1/2 cups fresh or frozen organic blueberries

1/2 cup fresh berries, such as strawberries, raspberries, or blackberries

Combine the juice and agar in a medium sauce pan. Bring to a boil, whisking frequently. Mix together the maple syrup and arrowroot until smooth. Whisk the arrowroot mixture until it thickens and returns to its original color. Add the fruit, stir well, and pour on top of the baked tofu in the pie crust. Allow to cool completely before serving. *Makes one 9-inch single-crust pie.*

WANDA'S PIE IN THE SKY

─ TORONTO, ONTARIO ─

The pies at Wanda's Pie in the Sky are seriously delicious pieces of heaven, and owner Wanda Beaver has witnessed firsthand the ardent cravings people get for a slice of old-fashioned pie. Toronto is home to a huge, annual film festival—second in prestige only to Cannes—and year after year during the September festival, Wanda serves pie to hotshot movie executives from L.A., some of whom come in more than once a day while they're in town. Puzzled by their insatiable appetite for pie, she realized that even though they've got big-time careers and live in a city where dining out at the trendiest restaurants is akin to a competitive sport, pie reminds them of their mothers, their grandmothers, and their youth.

Beaver traces her love of pie back to her childhood spent in Ontario's Niagara fruit-belt region, where at the age of nine, she baked her first cherry pie. Later, as a college student, she baked a peach pie for a friend whose roommate happened to manage a restaurant. The pie was a huge hit, and Beaver soon found herself abandoning her studies to bake pies for the roommate's restaurant. She transported the pies using a handheld carrier created by an industrial-design student, who later became her husband.

Beaver talks about pies with unadulterated love and a healthy dose of humor. She calls her lemon meringue pie the "Marilyn Monroe of pies: tart, blonde, and voluptuous." She encourages at-home bakers to be patient, as this pie, with its sky-high meringue and creamy filling, can be a bit tricky to master. The result of your labors, she promises, will be as unforgettable as Monroe herself.

Lemon Meringue Pie

Filling

    2 cups water

    1 cup sugar

    $1/2$ cup cornstarch

    5 egg yolks, beaten

    $1/4$ cup ($1/2$ stick) unsalted butter

    $3/4$ cup fresh lemon juice

    1 tablespoon grated lemon zest

    1 teaspoon vanilla extract

1 fully baked 10-inch pie shell (page 8)

Boil the water in a large saucepan and remove from the heat for 5 minutes. Whisk the sugar and cornstarch together. Add the mixture gradually to the water in the pan, whisking until completely incorporated. Cook over medium heat, whisking constantly, until the mixture comes to a boil and is thick. Add 1 cup of the hot mixture to the beaten egg yolks in a separate bowl, stirring until smooth. Whisking vigorously, add the yolk mixture to the pot and continue cooking, stirring constantly, until the mixture comes to a boil. Remove from heat and stir in the butter until well mixed. Add the lemon juice, zest, and vanilla, stirring until combined. Pour into the pie shell. Cover with plastic wrap and cool to room temperature.

Meringue

    5 egg whites, at room temperature

    $1/2$ teaspoon cream of tartar

    $1/4$ teaspoon salt

    $1/2$ teaspoon vanilla extract

    $3/4$ cup sugar

Preheat the oven to 375°F. Combine the egg whites, cream of tartar, salt, and vanilla extract, and beat with an electric mixer until soft peaks form. Gradually add the sugar and beat until stiff, glossy peaks form. Pile onto the cooled pie, bringing the meringue all the way over to the edge of the crust to seal the top completely. Bake for 15 to 20 minutes, or until golden. Cool on a wire rack and serve within 6 hours to avoid a soggy crust. *Makes one 10-inch single-crust pie.*

THE PIE PLATE BAKERY & CAFÉ

VIRGIL, ONTARIO

Smack in the middle of the Niagara fruit belt, the Pie Plate Bakery & Café is located right near orchards producing strawberries, raspberries, peaches, blueberries, cherries, apples, apricots, plums, and pears. Each morning, Pie Plate owner Ruth Anne Schriefer visits local farms to get her pick of the bounty for her bakery's pies. She loves bending recipes to her will and inventing new and sometimes unexpected fruit combinations. One common formula is pairing a sweet fruit, such as an apricot, with something a bit more tart, like a plum, then tossing some berries into the mix. (Blueberries are a good choice with apricots and plums.) She also suggests substituting orange zest for lemon zest, particularly when baking with strawberries, or adding finely chopped candied ginger when making a pie with pears or peaches. Golden raisins and nuts work well in apple pies, or sprinkle some sliced almonds or a handful of crumble mixture on the top of a pie about five minutes before pulling it out of the oven. Or don't. It's up to you!

The Pie Plate's recipe for a fresh fruit pie is a lot of fun because you can change it a little or a lot, resulting in a brand-new pie each time you make it. Schriefer suggests these combinations: strawberry-rhubarb, peach-plum-raspberry, apple-pear-raspberry, apple-apricot-rhubarb, and apricot-peach-blueberry.

Niagara Fresh Fruit Pie

Pie shell dough (page 8)

Preheat the oven to 450°F. Roll the dough into a 14-inch round and fit into a 9-inch pie plate, with the edges hanging over the side.

Filling

> $3/4$ cup granulated sugar, or $1/4$ cup packed brown sugar
>
> 2 tablespoons cornstarch
>
> 1 tablespoon tapioca flour
>
> $1/4$ teaspoon ground cinnamon
>
> 5 cups mixed sliced fresh fruit and berries
>
> $1/4$ teaspoon grated lemon zest
>
> 1 tablespoon unsalted butter, cut into bits

Cream, for brushing
Raw sugar, for sprinkling

Mix together the sugar, cornstarch, tapioca flour, and cinnamon, and sprinkle half in the pie shell. Toss the fruit and berries together with lemon zest and place on top of the sugar mixture in pie shell. Sprinkle the remaining sugar mixture over the fruit. Dot the butter on top. Fold the hanging pie dough up over the fruit. Brush with cream and sprinkle with raw sugar. Bake for 10 minutes. Reduce the oven temperature to 350°F and bake for 40 more minutes, or until the fruit is tender and juices bubble in the center. *Makes one 9-inch single-crust pie.*

GENERAL BAKIN' TIP

★ Schriefer (gasp!) typically does not peel her fruits before using them in her pies. Unless the fruit's skin is thick or too fuzzy, she says, leave it on to add more flavor. If you're using very juicy fruits, add an extra tablespoon of tapioca flour to offset the extra runniness.

SWEET CAROLINE

KINGSTON, ONTARIO

Carolyn Rundle once had aspirations of being a graphic designer, but, luckily for anyone who's ever tasted one of her sweet treats, she chose to work in culinary arts. Growing up in a section of Ontario known as the "apple bowl," where her grandparents owned an orchard, Rundle was surrounded by fresh fruit throughout her childhood. After working at a delicatessen and opening her own vegetarian restaurant in Kingston, Rundle decided to devote her time exclusively to dessert-making. She took a job as a pastry chef at Windmills Restaurant, also in Kingston, where dessert sales soon tripled and Rundle's following grew. She decided to become a "freelance" baker, opening her own business, Sweet Caroline, in 2003.

One of her favorite desserts to bake is the apple-cranberry galette with caramel. The difference between galettes and standard pies is minimal: Traditionally, galettes were baked on hot stones rather than in pans, and nowadays they are baked in conventional ovens on round pizza stones or pans. The dough is folded up over part of the filling and forms a pocket around the fruit. It's no surprise that the beloved apples of Rundle's youth end up in many of her desserts, and for this recipe, Rundle uses Northern Spy apples. Gravensteins work well, too. Rundle adds, "I love the freeform style of this pie. You can even patch it here and there, and it still looks great. The finishing touch of caramel is really easy and quick."

Apple-Cranberry Galette with Caramel

Crust

>   2 1/2 cups all-purpose flour
>   1/2 teaspoon salt
>   1/8 cup sugar
>   1/2 teaspoon baking powder
>   1/2 cup (1 stick) cold butter, cut into 1/2-inch cubes
>   1/2 cup cold vegetable shortening, cut into 1/2-inch cubes
>   1/4 cup cold water
>   1/4 cup sour cream

Whisk together the flour, salt, sugar, and baking powder. Cut in the butter and shortening. Combine the water and sour cream and add to the pastry mixture, mixing just until combined. Form into a disk, wrap in plastic, and refrigerate for 1 hour.

Filling

>   8 apples, peeled and cored
>   Mixed spices: 5 teaspoons ground coriander, 4 teaspoons ground cinnamon, 1/2 teaspoon *each* ground nutmeg, allspice, and ginger, 1/4 teaspoon *each* ground cloves and cardamom
>   2 tablespoons plus 1 1/2 cups sugar
>   1/2 cup orange juice
>   1 1/2 cups fresh or frozen cranberries
>   1 tablespoon grated orange zest
>   1 teaspoon vanilla extract
>   2 tablespoons all-purpose flour

Glaze: 1 egg and 1 tablespoon cream, mixed together

Thinly slice half the apples and place in a large bowl. Cut the remaining apples in half. Put the apple halves in a separate bowl and sprinkle with 1/2 teaspoon mixed spices, the 2 tablespoons sugar, and 1/4 cup orange juice. Set aside. Toss the sliced apples with the cranberries, the 1 1/2 cups of sugar, 1/4 cup orange juice, zest, 1 teaspoon mixed spices, vanilla, and flour. Set aside. Preheat the oven to 400°F. Roll the dough into an 18-inch round. Place on a lightly buttered 12-inch pizza pan. Pile the filling onto the dough. Place the apple halves around the circumference. Fold the dough over the apple halves. Glaze and bake for 1 hour. Drizzle with caramel, if desired. *Makes one 12-inch galette.*

Restaurant names are in *italic*.

A

Aberdeen Mansion (Vancouver, British Columbia), 96–97
Almond Chocolate Pie, Sadie's, 91
Apples
    Apple-Cranberry Galette with Caramel, 109
    Apple Pie, 39, 83
    New Mexican Apple Pie, 87
    Old-Fashioned Apple Pie, 23
    Sweet Apple Pie, 35
Arbor Hill Winery (Naples, New York), 20–21
Around the Clock Restaurant & Bakery (Crystal Lake, Illinois), 38–39

B

Bakery, 40
Baking, joy of, 6–7
Banana Cream Pie, 55
Bayona (New Orleans, Louisiana), 68–69
Berry (Very) Pie, 103
The Best Of (TV show), 46
Blackberries
    Peach-Blackberry Pie, 15
    Pear-Blackberry Pie with Cardamom, 19
    Very Berry Pie, 103
Black Cat Guest Ranch (Hinton, Alberta), 92–93
"Blind" baking, 9
Blueberries
    Very Berry Pie, 103
    Wild Blueberry Pie, 25
Blue Bonnet Café (Marble Falls, Texas), 62–63
Bob Andy Pie, 53
Bon Appétit, 12
The Border Grill (Santa Monica, California), 84
Boston magazine, 16
Butter (unsalted), 8
Butter Coffee Crunch Pie, 13

C

Cajeta, 82
Canada killer pies, 90–109
Caramel, Apple-Cranberry Galette with, 109
Cardamom, Pear-Blackberry Pie with, 19
Cascadia Bakery (Victoria, British Columbia), 98–99
Cherries
    Chocolate-Covered Cherry Pie, 47
    Door Country Cherry Pie, 31
    Raspberry Cherry Pie, 75
Chess pies
    Lemon Chess Pie, 57
    Old-Fashioned Chess Pie, 81
Cheyenne Ridge Outfitters & Lodge (Pierre, South Dakota), 32–33
Chocolate
    Chocolate-Covered Cherry Pie, 47
    Chocolate Pecan Pie, 79
    Fudge Pie, 65
    Grandma's Chocolate Pie, 73
    Mexican Chocolate Cream Pie, 85
    Sadie's Almond Chocolate Pie, 91
    S'more Pie, 69
Coconut
    Coconut Cream Pie, 62
    Coconut Meringue Pie, 61

Coffee Butter Crunch Pie, 13
Comfort Pie, Mississippi, 77
Concord Grape Pie, 21
Cooling pies, 9
Cranberry-Apple Galette with Caramel, 109
Cream pies
    Banana Cream Pie, 55
    Coconut Cream Pie, 62
    Mexican Chocolate Cream Pie, 85
    Walnut Cream Pie, 11
Crumb Pie, Plum-Strawberry, 17
Crusts, 8, 9
Crystal Grill (Greenwood, Mississippi), 60–61
Culinary Hall of Fame, 10
Cutting pies, 9

D

The Daily Pie Café (Pie Town, New Mexico), 86–87
Dangerously Delicious Pies (Baltimore, Maryland), 52–53
Decorative crust designs, 9
Deerfield's Bakery (Deerfield, Illinois), 40–41
Dessert Circus (TV show), 24
Door Country Cherry Pie, 31
Double-crust fruit pies, 9

E

Ed & Kay's (Benton, Arkansas), 64–65

F

The Famous Dutch Kitchen Restaurant (Frackville, Pennsylvania), 26–27
The Famous Plaza Café (Santa Fe, New Mexico), 82–83
Fats, 8–9
Fluting, 9
Food Network, 46, 66, 84
French Culinary Institute, 24
Fresh Fruit Pie, Niagara, 106, 107
Frozen Peanut Butter Pie, 97
Fruit (Niagara Fresh) Pie, 106, 107
Fudge Pie, 65

G

Galette (Apple-Cranberry) with Caramel, 109
The Golden Lamb (Lebanon, Ohio), 48–49
Gourmet, 10, 16
Grandma's Chocolate Pie, 73
Grape (Concord) Pie, 21

H

The Ham Shoppe (Valle Crucis, North Carolina), 50–51
Heartwood Bakery & Café (Halifax, Nova Scotia), 102–03

I

Ingredients and substitutions, 7
Inn at Schoolhouse Creek (Mendocino, California), 76–77

J

Johnny's Café (Omaha, Nebraska), 44–45
Johnny's Café Pecan Pie, 45
Just Desserts Café (Winnipeg, Manitoba), 94–95
Just Pies (Worthington, Ohio), 46–47

K

Kahlúa Pecan Pie, 59
Key Lime Pie, 67

L

Lange's Café (Pipestone, Minnesota), 36–37

Leaves, decorative crust design, 9

Lemon

Lemon Chess Pie, 57

Lemon Meringue Pie, 105

"Mile-High" Lemon Chiffon Pie, 43

Life, 42

Lime (Key Lime) Pie, 67

Little Pie Company (New York City, New York), 9, 22–23

Louie's Backyard (Key West, Florida), 66–67

Lynden Dutch Bakery (Lynden, Washington), 70–71

M

Manitoba Maple-Walnut Pie, 95

Maple

Manitoba Maple-Walnut Pie, 95

Maple Syrup Pie, 101

Marjolaine Pastry Shop (New Haven, Connecticut), 18–19

McEwen's on Monroe (Memphis, Tennessee), 54–55

Meringue

Coconut Meringue Pie, 61

Lemon Meringue Pie, 105

Mexican Chocolate Cream Pie, 85

Midwestern U.S. killer pies, 30–49

"Mile-High" Lemon Chiffon Pie, 43

Mississippi Comfort Pie, 77

Modern Bride, 68

Moody's Dinner (Waldoboro, Maine), 10–11

The Morrison-Clark Inn (Washington, District of Columbia), 56–57

N

National Geographic, 42

National Retail Bakery of the Year, 40

New Mexican Apple Pie, 87

New Orleans Culinary Concierge, 68

New York Daily News, 68

New York magazine, 24

Niagara Fresh Fruit Pie, 107

Northeastern U.S. killer pies, 10–29

Northern Alberta Institute of Technology, 90

North Fork Store & Café (North Fork, Idaho), 74–75

O

Old-Fashioned Apple Pie, 23

Old-Fashioned Chess Pie, 81

Oprah (TV show), 46

Ovens, 9

P

Peaches

Peach-Blackberry Pie, 15

Peach Pie, 89

Peanut Butter Pie, Frozen, 97

Pear-Blackberry Pie with Cardamom, 19

Pecans

Chocolate Pecan Pie, 79

Johnny's Café Pecan Pie, 45

Kahlúa Pecan Pie, 59

Pecan Pie, 41

Petsi Pies (Somerville, Massachusetts), 14–15

Pie In the Sky (Scottsdale, Arizona), 88–89

The Pie Plate Bakery & Café (Virgil, Ontario), 106–07

Pie plates (ceramic or glass), 9

Pies 101, baking tips, 8–9

The Plaza Restaurant (Santa Fe, New Mexico), 82–83

Plums

Plum-Strawberry Crumb Pie, 17

Sour Cream Plum Pie, 33

Ponzio's (Cherry Hill, New Jersey), 28–29

Ponzio's Pumpkin Pie, 29

Poogan's Porch (Charleston, South Carolina), 58–59

Pre-baking ("blind"), 9

Pumpkin Pie, Ponzio's, 29

R

Raisin Sour Cream Pie *(Lange's Café)*, 37

Raisin Sour Cream Pie *(Lynden Dutch Bakery)*, 71

Raspberries

Raspberry Cherry Pie, 75

Raspberry-Rhubarb Pie, 99

Very Berry Pie, 103

Restaurant Aux Anciens Canadiens (Quebec City, Quebec), 100–01

Rhubarb

Raspberry-Rhubarb Pie, 99

Strawberry-Rhubarb Pie, 51

Roadfood (Stern and Stern), 10, 60

Rose River Inn Bed & Breakfast (Astoria, Oregon), 72–73

S

Sadie's Almond Chocolate Pie, 91

Saskatoon Pie, 93

The Saturday Evening Post,, 42

Saveur, 10

The 1785 Inn (North Conway, New Hampshire), 12–13

Shaker Sugar Pie, Sister Lizzie's, 49

Shoofly Wet-Bottom Pie, 27

Sister Lizzie's Shaker Sugar Pie, 49

S'more Pie, 69

Sour cream

Sour Cream Plum Pie, 33

Sour Cream Raisin Pie *(Lange's Café)*, 37

Sour Cream Raisin Pie *(Lynden Dutch Bakery)*, 71

Southern U.S. killer pies, 50–69

Stagecoach Inn Bed & Breakfast (Cedarburg, Wisconsin), 34–35, 48

Stone's Restaurant (Marshalltown, Iowa), 42–43

Strawberries

Plum-Strawberry Crumb Pie, 17

Strawberry-Rhubarb Pie, 51

Very Berry Pie, 103

Sugar Pie (Shaker), Sister Lizzie's, 49

Sweet Apple Pie, 35

Sweet Caroline (Kingston, Ontario), 108–09

Sweetie Pies (Fish Creek, Wisconsin), 30–31

Sweetie Pies (Napa, California), 78–79

V

Verrill Farm (Concord, Massachusetts), 16–17

Very Berry Pie, 103

Vi's for Pies (Edmonton, Alberta), 90–91

W

Walnut Café (Boulder, Colorado), 80–81

Walnut Cream Pie, 11

Wanda's Pie In the Sky (Toronto, Ontario), 8, 104–05

Western U.S. killer pies, 70–89

Westville (New York City, New York), 24–25

Wet-Bottom Shoofly Pie, 27

Wild Blueberry Pie, 25

Wine Spectator, 66

ACKNOWLEDGMENTS

Thanks to all the chefs, bakers, and restaurant owners who generously shared their pie recipes and stories with me. This book would not be possible without you.

Thanks to Mom and Dad, Kate, Michael, Michelle, the Feuchtenbergers, the Findlings, the Andersons, the Czaplickis, the Encks, the Bohns, the Witmers, the Blakes, Jon, Sarah and Tim, Charlie, Christy, the Shippensburg University English Department, my students past and present, and all of my friends and family for their kind and steadfast support.

Thanks to Kasey Free, Meghan Cleary, and everyone at becker&mayer!. Extra-special thanks to my editor, Kate Perry, for giving me this wonderful job and for your much-appreciated (and needed!) advice, guidance, and encouragement. I couldn't have done it without you.

Thanks to everyone at Chronicle Books.

Most of all, thanks and love to Scott. You are sweeter than any pie.

IMAGE CREDITS

OTHER TASTY COOKBOOKS IN THE *Killer* SERIES

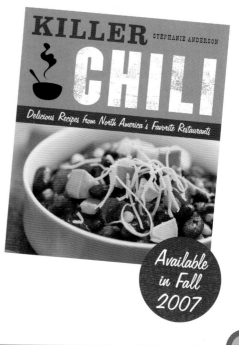

Spanning from east to west, Texas to Toronto, and countless spots in between, the acclaimed *Killer Ribs* serves up smokin' recipes for the most succulent sauces, spiciest rubs, and juiciest ribs you've ever tasted. From tangy, slow-roasted baby backs and sweet pineapple loin-back pork ribs to zesty black pepper beef ribs and citrus-laden alligator ribs, every delicious region is represented. Whether you're a seasoned barbecue enthusiast or a hungry greenhorn, you'll be inspired to create these tempting dishes cooked up by award-winning chefs from every corner of the continent.

$16.95 ISBN-10: 1-932855-37-8; ISBN-13: 978-1-932855-37-1

Killer Chili presents the best, most appetizing chili recipes from fifty renowned restaurants in the United States and Canada. Wherever your taste preferences fall on the chili spectrum—poblano and grilled chicken, truly unique bison, rosemary-flavored Tuscan, Southwestern black bean, or even Maine style—this mouthwatering volume contains old favorites, exotic new twists, and other exciting varieties sure to satisfy your desire for a steaming bowl of "red." The passionate chili aficionados in the third cookbook of the *Killer* series have developed unique and bona fide methods for the best bowl-filling fare you can find.

$16.95 ISBN-10: 1-932855-60-2; ISBN-13: 978-1-932855-60-9